AF333893

Essays on Faith and Culture

Essays on Faith and Culture

✠ ✠ ✠

V. Rev. Leonidas Contos
Sir Dimitri Obolensky
Eva Catafygiotu Topping
Speros Vryonis, Jr.

Compiled by
Anton C. Vrame, Ph.D.
and
Cory C. Dixon

InterOrthodox Press
Berkeley, California

© Copyright 2003
Published by InterOrthodox Press
Patriarch Athenagoras Orthodox Institute
2311 Hearst Avenue
Berkeley, CA 94709

ISBN 1-932401-01-6

All rights reserved. No part of this book may be reproduced, stored in a retrieval system, or transmitted in any form or by any means, electronic, mechanical, photocopying, recording, or otherwise without the prior permission of the publisher.

Library of Congress Cataloging-in-Publication Data

Essays on faith and culture / compiled by Anton C. Vrame and Cory C. Dixon.
        p. cm.
Includes bibliographical references.
    ISBN 1-932401-01-6 (pbk.)
 1. Christianity and culture. 2. Tradition (Theology) 3. Women in the Orthodox Eastern Church. 4. Orthodox Eastern Church--Doctrines. I. Vrame, Anton C. II. Dixon, Cory C., 1979-
BR115.C8E77 2003
261--dc22
                                        2003018585

Contents

Editor's Note

The topic of faith and culture has been of particular concern to Orthodox Christianity. As Professor Vryonis points out in his essay included in this volume, the topic was "one of the burning issues in the early church." Tertullian's question "What has Athens to do with Jerusalem?" best sums up the problem.

In our day, many theologians, such as Fr. John Meyendorff and Fr. John Romanides repeatedly turned to the question. In North America, the topic is often lively because of its immediacy. The interaction of Orthodox Christianity, ethnic identity, and cultural assimilation to the American milieu has created challenges on multiple levels. To name a few: the challenges of multiple ethnic jurisdictions, translations of services into English, the influx of persons embracing Orthodox Christianity from outside traditional groups, creating the phenomenon of so-called "cradle Orthodox" and the convert.

The topic was picked up in the early days of the Patriarch Athenagoras Orthodox Institute (PAOI). Unfortunately the Institute does not possess all the talks that were delivered here, notably the lectures of Ware, Meyendorff, and Pelikan, which, based on their titles, also dealt with the issue in one way or another. Undoubtedly and is frequently the case, those lectures appeared in other publications. However, those that we do possess on this topic are included in this volume. Despite the age of some of the papers, they deserve dissemination and careful study.

The eminent Byzantine scholar Speros Vryonis dealt with

it in his panegyric speech at the 1987 dedication of the Alexander Spanos Chair in Orthodox Christian Studies at the Graduate Theological Union, the ecumenical consortium to which the PAOI belongs. In his speech, Professor Vryonis looks closely at the issue in the early church, focusing especially on St. Basil the Great's *Address to youth*. Professor Vryonis, a good friend of the Institute and one-time Trustee, was Alexander S. Onassis Professor of Hellenic Civilization and Director of the Onassis Center for Hellenic Studies at New York Univerity, at the time of his presentation.

Sir Dimitri Obolensky is well known to historians and theologians for his ideas about the "Byzantine commonwealth." His three-part presentation, was originally delivered as the Fifth Distinguished Lecture series of the PAOI. Here Obolensky explores aspects of Slavic Christianity's cultural relationship with Byzantium. As one might expect, the relationship has points of convergence and points of tension.

Fr. Leonidas Contos' presentation was originally made to members of the Archbishop Iakovos Leadership 100 Endowment Fund in 1995. Fr. Contos' presentation deals with the challenging task of translating the richness of the Orthodox Tradition, especially its liturgical heritage, for the modern believer. He explores how traditions are preserved through the art of the translator. Contos' presentation was not delivered in the context of the Institute, but Fr. Leon's legacy at the Institute is palpable and deserves a place here. Also, Fr. Contos fell asleep in the Lord later that year; thus this presentation may be one of his last public presentations.

Eva Topping's paper explores how antiquated cultural values have influenced ecclesial practices in the treatment of women in the Church. Delivered at the Institute in 1988, a reader would hope that these issues have been resolved. While there has been some progress, the basic issues about the status of women in the Orthodox Church remain.

A note about the essays. Given the diverse nature of the presentations, from Distinguished Lectures to other venues, we have not tried to "edit out" any inconsistencies in style or citations. Rather, we have kept each presentation intact, as it was presented originally. My thanks go to Mr. Cory Dixon, a graduate student at The University of Chicago Divinity School for his painstaking efforts to prepare and check the manuscripts of each presentation.

Anton C. Vrame, Ph.D.
Editor

The Orthodox Church and Culture

Speros Vryonis, Jr.

In ancient Greece auspicious events were the occasion for the panegyric discourse, the *logos panegyrikos*. We are gathered this evening to celebrate such an auspicious event, and so, in accordance with the laws of discourse governing the *logos panegyrikos*, we acclaim the dedication of the Patriarch Athenagoras Orthodox Institute and the Inauguration of the Alexander G. Spanos Chair of Orthodox Thought and Culture. Further, the *logos panegyrikos* acclaims the creator of the auspicious event. Alexander, you have created a treasured possession for eternity – *ktema te es aei*— as Thucydides first said, for a chair as you know is, by the very act of its legal creation, an entity in the eyes of the law whose goal and scope may never be changed. You have, thus, founded a chair of learning which is eternal and which will forever dispense knowledge of Orthodox thought and culture – *aenos pege*, an everflowing spring. The *logos panegyrikos* also praises the host of the newly created chair, the Graduate Theological Union and the Patriarch Athenagoras Orthodox Institute, for the breadth and progressive character of its spirit in bringing the strain of Orthodox thought and culture within the scope of its ever widening goals. Now, the *logos panegyrikos* congratulates the first holder of the Alexander G. Spanos chair, the Very Reverend Dr. Leonidas Contos, and exhorts him to bring his many and rich talents to the challenge before him and to bring the results which we expect from him and the Chair. Finally, the *logos panegyrikos* demands a didactic moral drawn from an ancient and learned author which will instruct the assembly and which will exhort it appropriately.

The Statement of Mission of the Patriarch Athenagoras Orthodox Institute states in its very first paragraph the specific goal of the Institute: "To become an important center for the study and dissemination of Orthodox thought and culture." In so doing it sets as its area of activity not only theology (thought) but the much broader and more inclusive dimension of culture. This is commendable inasmuch as Orthodox thought or theology can best be understood within the broader context of the culture within which dogmatic thought arose and developed.

The term culture, today, as applied by anthropology, is all inclusive containing within it all the manifestations, concepts, institutions and activities of the life of an extended society, both material and cognitive. It includes such diverse aspects of man's activity as politics, science, religious concepts and organizations, art, crafts, agriculture, music, etc.[1]

By this definition the founders of the Patriarch Athenagoras Orthodox Institute have given its program the widest possible scope and have assured that structure which will deal with the Orthodox tradition in the broadest and richest manner possible. The phrase "Orthodox thought and culture" thus raises the problem of the historical relations of the Orthodox Church to culture broadly defined. What was, historically, the attitude of the Orthodox Church to culture? Was it a homogenous and uniform attitude? Did it come to terms with the culture within which it first spread? In examining this question we shall not

---

[1] A. L. Koreber and C. Kluckohn, *Culture: A Critical Review of Concepts and Definitions*. (New York, n.d.).

merely confront the fundamental question of the Orthodox Church's relation to culture in earlier times, but we shall also see what tradition it has inherited presently, and how this tradition could orient Orthodox thought and culture to western culture today, something particularly relevant to the newly created Patriarch Athenagoras Orthodox Institute.

The problem of the relation of the Orthodox Church to culture was one of the burning issues in the early church. The basic question, *'What does Athens have to do with Jerusalem'*, occasioned continuing strife, uncertainty and ambivalence, from earliest times. For, when Christianity spread into the Graeco-Roman world it came into contact with a world whose very thought and existence, to say nothing of its art, literature, education and everyday life, were permeated by polytheism and by a system of thought which left great room for metaphysical speculation. Whereas this polytheism and relative freedom of thought constituted essentials in a culture within which Christianity had to spread, at the same time, however, they constituted basic oppositions to the Hebraic tradition of monotheism on the one hand, and the superiority of divine revelation and prophetic books over the freely exercised logic of the human mind on the other.

Very soon there arose a strong tradition of austere Christians who abhorred pagan learning and literature as antithetical to these two basic characteristics of the Christian religion, just as in the beginning there was also a reluctance to admit the human figure in Christian decorational arts. This tradition remained strong, particularly within the monastic domain of the Orthodox Church well into the Christian period and beyond. The ninth century hagiographer of his contemporary St. John Psichaites writes boastfully of the education of the Abbot John:

He had no need of (knowing) the agreement of words and phrases and the details of language (grammar), neither of losing himself in the grammatical minutiae nor of learning the nonsense of Homer, his golden chain, or the art of harnessing and unharnessing the chariot . . . . What profit can those who take pride in such derive from the knowledge of these myths, fictions and satanic inventions?

The hagiographer continues:

He has no need of the lies of orators. He treated astronomy, geometry and arithmetic as things without real existence.

As for Plato:

He slithers in the mire of passions, his belly full and a parasite.[2]

Leo the Mathematician, a contemporary of St. John Psichaites and the head of the newly refounded University of Constantinople in 855/6, was attacked by one of his students, the monk Constantine, as a paganizer who had abandoned Christ. Upon his death Constantine wrote that his teacher had descended to hell where he was now in the company of Chrysippus, Epicurus, Plato, Aristotle, and Socrates.[3]

Thus we see that not only ancient literature but the ancient systems of education (*egkyklios paideia*) and thought were savagely attacked by many Byzantine Empire churchmen. Indeed, at the very end of the Byzantine Empire, the Patriarch

---

[2] For these texts, S. Vryonis, "*Cultural Conformity in Byzantine Society,*" in *Individualism and Conflict in Classical Islam*, ed. A. Banani and S. Vryonis, Fifth Giogio Levi della Vida Biennial Conference (Wiesbaden, 1977), 132-133.

[3] Vryonis, op. Cit., 133.

Gennadios Scholarios burned the works of Pletho in which the latter had laid out a plan for the revival of the pagan religion among the Greeks.[4] But parallel to this anti-Hellenism within the Orthodox Church there was a very powerful current of what we might call, for lack of a better term, philhellenism, that is a great love for and exercise in ancient Greek literature and education. Here one could merely point to St. John Psichaites' contemporary the Patriarch Photios, the great classicist of the Macedonian Renaissance, and to Bessarion the metropolitan of Trebizond and contemporary of Gennadios Scholarios. Bessarion was a pupil of the pagan Pletho and the creator of the great and very important collection of manuscripts of classical Greek authors which constitutes the prize and glory of the Bibliotheca Marciana in Venice.[5]

By the end of the fourth century the fathers of the Orthodox Church had met head on the challenge of contemporary culture and had arrived at a solution to accommodate the older pagan Greek culture and their own Judaeo-Christian message. In so doing they found a working compromise which permitted the co-existence of both in varying degrees, but which at the same time greatly changed both these traditions within the Byzantine civilization. The basic outlines of this fundamental encounter were masterfully sketched by the late Werner Jaeger

[4] Vryonis, "*Crises and Anxieties in Fifteenth Century Byzantium: and the Reassertion of Old, and the Emergency of New, Cultural Forms,*" in *Islamic and Middle Eastern Societies,* ed. R. Olson (Brattelboro, 1988), 120-123; "*The Freedom of Expression in Fifteenth Century Byzantium,*" in G. Makdisi and D. Sourdel, eds., *La notion de liberté au Moyen Age. Islam, Byzance, Occident. The International Colloquium of Morigny (France), Byzantium, Islam, and the Latin West in the Middle Ages,* Proceedings no. IV (Paris, 1985), 261-273.
[5] H. Hunger, *Die Hochsprachliche Profane Literatur der Byzantiner* (Munich, 1978), I, 31. P. Lemerle, *Le premier humanisme byzantin. Notes et remarques sur enseignement et culture a Byzance des origines au Xe siecles* (Paris, 1971), 185ff.

in his remarkable little book on the subject wherein he established the structures and rhythms that saw the accommodation of Christianity and Greek culture. By culture Jaeger of course did not intend the broader anthropological definition but a narrower one which focused on aspects of formal culture, that is literature, philology, philosophy, and scholarship. In these, of course, the basic stages included the decision to present the Christian message in the Greek language, a language which brought with it an entire philosophical and civilizational raiment. It included also the apologists, the school of Alexandria which as heir to the traditions of Hellenistic scholarship allied this Greek philological and interpretative scholarship to the formulation of Christian dogma and holy texts. Finally it ends with the Christian humanism of the Cappadocian fathers.[6]

Perhaps the most incisive and clear exposition of the creation of what some have termed this Christian humanism in the early church is the address of St. Basil of Caesarea (329/331-379)[7] entitled 'Address to the youth as to how they might profit from Greek literature'.

In this discourse Basil addresses a young audience and exhorts it to profit from the writings of the ancient Greeks, but to do so according to the rules which Christian conscience, or Christian wisdom, dictates.

Basil first admonishes the young audience to heed his words and advice for as a man of mature years, as a man who has experienced much and thus been through the school of life, he is well qualified to point out the safest road for all those setting out on life.[8] Thus, says Basil, what he has to say has practical application, it is not some idle theoretical exercise. And with

---

[6] W. Jaeger, *Early Christianity and Greek Paideia* (Oxford, 1969).
[7] P. J. Fenwick, ed., *Basil of Caesarea. Christian, Humaist, Ascetic. A Sixteen-hundredth Anniversary Symposium.* (Toronto, 1981), I-II.
[8] Basil, "Address to the Youth", I.1.

this he immediately plunges into the subject of his exhortation:

> Do not be amazed if I say to you who come daily to a teacher and who make contact with the famous (elegant) men of antiquity through the remnants of their literary works, that I have found something useful (there) for myself. It is this precisely about which I now advise you. You must not unreservedly surrender, as one would not surrender the rudders of a ship, your minds or yourselves to wherever they might lead them, but you should accept from them what is useful (chrisimon) and you should know what one should disregard. Which these are and how we distinguish (them) is what I shall straightforth teach you.[9]

In order to provide the youth with the touchstone on what is useful and what is not, in the body of Greek literature and education, he states a basic principle at the beginning of his speech, which is the following:

> O children, we do not consider human life to be of any value, nor is it a good. For its utility is limited to this period of life.[10] Moreover we do not consider great or desirable bodily strength, beauty, size, honors, not even imperial rule itself, or indeed any other human matter, nor do we esteem those who possess them. For we go far beyond these things in our hopes and we make all our preparations for another life. That which is of advantage to us in this (other life) we say it is necessary to love and to pursue with all our strength, and that we should dispose of all those things which do not lead to that (other) life.[11]

---

[9] Basil, II, 1.
[10] Basil, II, 1.
[11] Basil, II, 2-3.

Basil admonishes his audience that the nature of this other life needs a longer discussion and at another time, as this discussion is for an *older* audience that will be better equipped to comprehend it. The difference between these two lives is comparable to the superiority of the soul over the body.

It is precisely because maturity and preparatory education are needed in order to study the holy mysteries, that the youth must begin with non-religious writings. These latter are thus categorized as Christian *propaideia*.

> It is the Holy Books which lead to this life by teaching us the mysteries. But since we are not of the age to understand the depth of (their) meaning, we exercise ourselves by means of the soul's eye, as in shadows and mirrors, imitating those who study the books of military tactics. For these latter acquire expertise by gesticulation of the hands and movements of the feet and so reap their profit during the battles. We must also realize that there lies ahead of us a contest which is the greatest of all contests and on behalf of which we must do and suffer everything, commensurate with our strength, in order to prepare for it; one must associate with poets, historians, orators, and with all men from whom advantage might derive as to the care of the soul. Just as the dyers having first prepared with some treatment whatever object is to receive the dye, then they apply the color . . . so also do we in the same manner, if we wish that the ideas of the good should remain indelibly imprinted in us, first absorb these pagan books, and then we shall understand the sacred and secret teachings. And as though having been accustomed to see the sun (in the reflection) of the water, we shall thus cast our sight on the light itself.[12]

Subsequently, Basil attempts to buttress his argument on

---

[12] Basil, II, 6-8.

not only the utility of pagan learning, but also on its propaideutic necessity, by reference to logic and to imagery. In discussing the two types of literature/education, pagan and Christian, Basil proposes that in the case where there is indeed some affinity of content between the two it would be useful for a better understanding of the latter to know the former. But even in the case where there might be no affinity between the two, a parallelism of the two would serve further to show us what is good and what is bad. He then shifts to the arboreal image in order to show the interrelated functionality of the two literatures. A tree has its virtue to be covered by fruit in season, and yet there is grace in enveloping it with pagan wisdom (*thyrathen sophia*) just as the leaves provide protection for the fruit and ornament for the tree. Finally, Basil bolsters his proposition in this third paragraph by reference to Biblical tradition: Moses had exercised his mind in the sciences of Egypt before entering upon a contemplation of God; Daniel had learned the wisdom of the Chaldees before devoting himself to the Divine teachings.[13]

Proceeding on the assumption that it is virtue that man must accumulate in order to save his soul in the next world, he ties the acquisition of virtue to a study of pagan literature.

Basil, in continuing to inform his young audience, is aware that the unrestrained study and imitation of the entirety of Greek literature can be seductive and can lead to a way of life that will not result in virtue and so will endanger the soul of the Christian. Thus, in part four he becomes specific as to what should be read, what should be imitated, and what should be avoided. Beginning with the poets, as did the ancient Greeks in the education of their own youth, Basil warns the neophytes that inasmuch as the poets display great variety we should not pay attention to all of them:

---

[13] Basil, III, 1-4.

When, however, they recount to you the deeds or sayings of good men, you shall love and imitate them and
try to be like them. But when they described the ras-
cally, one must avoid them, blocking one's ears no less
than they say Odysseus did against the songs of the
Seirenes. For becoming accustomed to evil books is a
road to the deeds (themselves). Thus the soul must be
guarded with all care, lest we accept unawares something evil because of the pleasure of the books, just as
those who accept poison with honey.[14]

On the other hand:

We shall not . . . praise the poets in all things (we do
not praise them when) they abuse, jeer, when they por-
tray loves or drunkards . . . . Least of all we heed them
they discourse on the gods, and particularly when they
speak of many of them and that they do not agree . . .
. We shall leave for the theater the adulteries of the
gods, their loves and open intercourses, and those especially of the chief and highest of them all, Zeus . . .
which if one were to relate in regard to livestock he
would blush.[15] And I would say these same things in
regard to the historians, especially when they compose
for the sake of amusement of the audience. Further we
shall not imitate the lying art of the orators. Indeed
the lie is not advantageous to those of us who have
chosen the correct and true path in life, neither in the
courts nor in other affairs.[16] We shall rather accept those
writings in which they praised virtue or attacked wick-
edness.[17]

St. Basil drives home his point by shifting to the charming

---

[14] Basil, IV, 2-3.
[15] Basil, IV, 4-5.
[16] Basil, IV, 6.
[17] Basil, IV, 7.

image of the bee and the flowers. For some, he says, the enjoyment of the flowers goes no further than the aromas of colors. But the bee also derives honey from the flowers. So with this pagan literature, there are those who derive the sweet and joyous from it, whereas others derive in addition, and store it away, profit for the soul (virtue).

> Accordingly we can profit (from this pagan literature) according to the image of the bee. For they (bees) neither alight on all flowers, nor do they attempt to take away everything from those flowers on which they do alight, but having taken away whatever is correct for their labor, they bid farewell to the rest.[18]

Since it is necessary to save up treasures for the next life, and since this can be done only by the acquisitions of virtue (*arete*), since the poets, historians, and especially the philosophers have praised virtue, and since the youth are unprepared for the ultimate Christian teaching, it follows that they must study these ancient authors in order to acquire virtue. For it is of no small profit, says Basil, that a certain familiarity and custom be born in the souls of the young from the lessons taught by the ancient authors, since lessons learned at an early age are indelibly impressed in the youth and remain immutable.[19] Did not Hesiod relate that the road leading to virtue is narrow, rugged and uphill? Further, all of the poetry of Homer constitutes an encomium of virtue. And Solon stated that we do not exchange our virtue for wealth, as virtue is eternal and riches are temporary. With these and other references Basil reinforces his argument and recapitulates it in a homiletic manner:

[18] Basil, IV, 8.
[19] Basil, V, 5-10.

> Nearly all those ancient authors who have a reputation for wisdom have praised virtue.[20] It is necessary to hear them and to attempt to demonstrate their words in our lives.[21]

The Cappadocian church father finally lends variety, and a certain humor, to his proof and discourse by selecting specific examples of virtue displayed by ancient Greeks and reported in this pagan literature, and which are at the same time parallel to specific Christian virtues. In the first case Pericles is said to have been the target of particularly violent abuse in the agora from one of the Athenian citizens. The statesman did not attempt to defend himself and when nightfall eventually forced the agitated Athenian to desist and to return home, Pericles provided him with torch bearers to see him home safely.[22] On a different occasion Socrates was physically, and violently, beaten about the face by a drunkard. The philosopher did not resist him, but allowed him to proceed about his violence. After having allowed the inebriated assailant to transform his face, Socrates satisfied himself merely by placing a sign on his forehead, much as sculptors did on their statues, saying. "So and so sculpted me." To our author this is an obvious parallel to the Christian injunction to turn the other cheek.[23] Finally, Alexander is praised for having not only forborne the pleasure of congress with the beautiful daughters of the conquered and slain Darius, but even to enjoy their sight. This is parallel, for Basil to Matthew V, 28, that even the thought constitutes adultery.[24]

So much for Basil's *Address to the youth as to how they might profit from Greek literature,* "and its charming array of images of

---

[20] Basil, V, 14.
[21] Basil, VI, 1.
[22] Basil, VII, 2-4.
[23] Basil, VII, 5-7.
[24] Basil VII, 8.

bees and flowers, trees, fruit and leaves, dyers and their craft, navigators and ships, soldiers and military manuals, Odysseus and the Seirenes, poison and honey. Behind this graceful literary imagery and the classical allusions (of 67 literary allusions, 57 are from pagan Greek authors – 19 from Plato alone – and only ten come from the Scriptures and the Church Fathers) lies the mind of Basil the Realist. For him Christian teaching could be studies and understood only following a training in pagan Greek literature and in the pagan educational system.[25] Further, the attainment of Christian virtue necessitated a pagan Greek *propaideia*. In Basil the Orthodox Church understood that it must come to terms with the living culture of its environment and in so doing should take, selectively, what is useful – *to chrisimon*. A cultural anthropologist would have said that in this respect Basil was a functionalist. Basil's address to the youth thus contains a remarkably creative and realistic spirit which has surfaced, periodically, in the Orthodox Church in its relations to other contemporary cultures. Its relevance and challenge to the Institute which has so recently been created, and from which we expect much, are obvious.

[25] H. I. Marrou, *A History of Education in Antiquity* (New York, 1964), passim.

Byzantium & Slavic Christianity: Influence or Dialogue?

Sir Dimitri Obolensky

THE PROCESS OF ACCULTURATION

The title I have chosen for these three lectures is concerned with a relationship and a question. The relationship is one between Byzantium and Slavic Christianity. These two terms are clearly fixed in space and time: they point to Eastern Europe and, in the main, to the Middle Ages. Their relationship will form the substance of these lectures; and, in an attempt to describe it historically, I will invite you to consider whether "influence" or "dialogue", or indeed any other term, is more appropriate.

Let me first consider the historical context within which the relationship between Byzantium and Slavic Christianity can be most usefully explored. In a book published some twenty years ago I argued that in the Middle Ages, despite notable differences in social and political life, those East European countries which owed their religion and much of their culture to Byzantium formed a single international community: its nature, I argued, is revealed in a common cultural tradition accepted by their ruling and educated classes. They were bound by the same profession of Eastern Christianity; they acknowledged the primacy of the Church of Constantinople; they recognized—at least tacitly—that the Byzantine Emperor was endowed with a measure of authority over the whole of Orthodox Christendom; they accepted the norms of Romano-Byzantine law; and they held that the literary standards and artistic techniques of the Empire's schools, monasteries and workshops were of universal validity and worthy of imitation. The Byzantine heritage of these East European countries was, I believed—and I still do—a significant enough component of their medieval tradition to justify the view that, in some respects, they formed a single international community. This community I called the Byzantine Commonwealth.

It was more difficult to define the boundaries of this community, for the geographical area inhabited by the European "heirs of Byzantium" altered in the course of time, expanding in some regions, contracting in others. Its heartland was the Balkan peninsula, the home of the Greeks, the Bulgarians, the Serbs, and the Albanians. In the ninth and tenth centuries it came to include Rus' (in modern terms Ukraine, Belarus, and Russia), and in the late Middle Ages the Roumanian lands as well. For several centuries, moreover, Byzantine civilization had some impact on both sides of the middle Danube, and thus influenced the early medieval culture of the Moravians, the Czechs, and the Hungarians. The notion of "Eastern Europe," which I have used here to cover all these regions, is little more than a loose empirical category obtained by combining a geographical with a cultural criterion. It thus excludes Poland, whose culture since the early Middle Ages has depended on the Latin world, as well as—regrettably—Venice, Sicily, and the Caucasian lands which, though they lay for centuries within the cultural orbit of Byzantium, fall outside Eastern Europe.

That the concept of the Byzantine Commonwealth provides a helpful context for viewing the relations between Byzantium and the Slavic Orthodox lands will, I hope, become clear as these lectures proceed. The same, I believe, applies to the two alternative terms in the title: "influence" and "dialogue."

In 1989 there appeared a study by the Russian linguist and semioticist Yury Lotman. Its Russian title is *Problema vizantiiskogo vliyaniya na russkuyu kul'turu v tipologicheskom osveshchenii*.[1] A rough English translation would be "The problem of the Byzantine influence on Russian culture viewed typologically." It is worth noting that the term "influence" (*vliyanie*) which occurs in its title gives way in the main body of his article to the term "dialogue." This simple, yet expressive, word may prove helpful in describing the encounter between Byzantium and the Slav societies of Eastern Europe. Lotman's gloss on this term seems to me of interest. In the opening stages of the dialogue, he states, "The first participant (the transmitter, *peredayushchy*) possesses a larger supply of accumulated experience (that is, memory), while the second participant (the receiver, *prinimayushchy*) is interested in acquiring this experience." Or, to quote another telling passage in Lotman's article, "In the beginning of the dialogue the dominant side, claiming for itself the central position in the cultural *oikoumene*, forces the receiver into a peripheral position." Thus, as you will see, Lotman does not wholly reject the term "influence"; yet he clearly prefers "dialogue."

Now Lotman's interpretation, in the present context, of the term "dialogue" brings to mind another technical term which is relevant to the subject of these lectures. It is "acculturation". The term has had a chequered history since about 1929, when it became popular among American anthropologists. Viewed at first with distrust by historians, especially in Europe, who disliked its imperialist, neo-colonialist, asso-

---

[1] Yu. M. Lotman, *Izbrannye stat'i*, I (Talinn, 1992), pp. 121–8.

ciations—not to mention its lack of euphony—it was given a tentative accolade in 1965, when it figured, as the title of one of the main themes, in the programme of the Twelfth International Congress of Historical Studies in Vienna. One of its original sponsors, Melville Herskovits, had defined acculturation as comprehending "those phenomena which result when groups of individuals having different cultures come into continuous first-hand contact, with subsequent changes in the original cultural patterns of either or both groups."[2] Another distinguished American cultural anthropologist, Alfred Kroeber, made the following distinction between acculturation and cultural diffusion: "When we follow the fortunes of a particular cultural trait or complex or institution through its meanderings from culture to culture, we call it a study of diffusion. When we consider two cultures bombarding each other with hundreds or thousands of diffusing traits, and appraise the results of such interaction, we more commonly call it acculturation. Diffusion is a matter of what happens to elements or parts of culture; acculturation, of what happens to cultures."[3]

The historian, while noting these comprehensive sociological definitions, may well prefer another description of acculturation, proposed by Alphonse Dupront in his introductory paper, presented to the Vienna Congress of historians. In translation it reads: "Acculturation is the movement of an individual, of a group, of a society, even of a culture towards another culture, therefore a dialogue, an education, a confrontation, a mingling, and more often than not a trial of strength."[4] This historian's definition, with its sense of the con-

---

[2] M. J. Herskovits, *Man and His Works* (New York, 1950), p. 523.
[3] A. L. Kroeber, *Anthropology* (New York, 1948), p. 425.
[4] "De l'Acculturation", *XIIe Congrès international des Sciences Historiques, Rapports, I: Grands Thèmes* (Vienna, 1965), p. 8.

crete, its suggestion of a variety of situations, and its intimations of complex and dramatic human experience, provides, I suggest, the most helpful starting point to a study of the encounter between Byzantium and the Slavic world of the Middle Ages. At the very least it can point the way to some of the things we should be looking for.

In the first place, movement. Byzantine civilization, as it expanded westward and northward across seas and plains, along river valleys and trade routes, and over mountain passes, may be likened to beams of light sent out from the Empire's cultural centres to the farthest regions of Eastern Europe. The Byzantine Empire, a sea-power during much of its history, inherited the trade relations which, since remote antiquity, had linked the Mediterranean with western Asia and continental Europe. The alternate movements of commodities, men and ideas to and from the Mediterranean world, which the great French historian Fernand Braudel compared to the rhythmic pulsations of the living heart,[5] brought the periphery of this world into close contact with its centres on the Bosphorus and the Aegean, and carried the civilization of Byzantium up rivers, across plains and over seas to the farthest borderlands of Eastern Europe.

This cultural movement, we shall see, was seldom in one direction only: in the history of the encounter between Byzantium and the Slavs there are many examples showing that the Slavs actively "reached out" for elements of Byzantine civilization and, when these became available to them, made a selection among them, accepting, rejecting, or transforming them.

The role played by movement in the process of accultura-

---

[5] F. Braudel, *La Méditerranée et le monde méditerranéen à l'époque de Philippe II* (Paris, 1949), p. 556.

tion, to be fully understood, requires a knowledge of historical geography. As far as Eastern Europe is concerned, this subject is now only beginning to be studied adequately. I will confine myself here to a few brief remarks about frontier zones. A distinction can probably be drawn between borderlands which divided societies of comparable cultural level, such as the Byzantine-Arab frontier, where a state of relative cultural equilibrium could be expected to prevail, and those between the Empire and less developed peoples, such as the Slavs. Across this type of frontier the encounter between civilization and barbarism (to use Byzantine concepts) took place mainly in conditions of cultural imbalance, in which the movement was more intense. To borrow another simile from Fernand Braudel, the greater the difference in voltage, the more powerful the current. Its intensity, and its speed, were also affected by distance and physical barriers, by the latter more than the former. So long as the society and culture of the Empire's northern neighbours remained on a primitive level, Byzantine influence was exerted upon them mainly at short range, across a frontier which, though never entirely closed, was still a frontier. But as the East European nations developed more complex and sophisticated cultures of their own, especially after the ninth century, distance began to play a diminishing role, and Byzantine cultural traits were carried across large intervening expanses of land and sea. They were halted far more effectively by mountain barriers. Many a community that dwelt in or behind the more inaccessible mountains of the Balkan peninsula remained for centuries scarcely affected by the surrounding culture; and in these cases the diffusion of Byzantine civilization, especially when it was further slowed down or interrupted by the resistance of these communities, resembled less the continuous beam of a searchlight than the faint glimmering of a distant star. The

Pindus and the Rhodopes, for instance, were far less affected in the Middle Ages by Byzantine influences than the far away city of Novgorod in northern Russia.

Let me remind you of the other factors included in Dupront's definition of acculturation: next to movement he listed dialogue, education, confrontation, mingling, and trial of strength. The most obvious, perhaps, is education. It needs no specialized knowledge to realize that in the realms of religion and law, literature and art the East European peoples—Slavs and Roumanians—were the pupils of Byzantium; and, in addition to the Empire's cultural exports, products of luxury and technological skill were avidly borrowed from Byzantium by their ruling classes. I shall have more to say on this subject in subsequent lectures. Here too, however, we must not forget that, in its new peripheral environment, Byzantine civilization was nearly always adapted to local needs and conditions. In discussing the process of cultural transmission, Simon Franklin of Cambridge University recently developed the concept of "cultural blockage." Though he applies it to the relations between Byzantium and Russia, it can equally be applied to other Slavic peoples. "An imaginary filter between Byzantium and Kiev", Franklin writes, "imposes what might be termed *cultural blockage*. Some material clogs in the filter and never reaches Russia; some passes through, but is so mangled that it is near useless; and some passes through relatively unscathed."[6] In this sense at least, the process of acculturation was indeed a *dialogue* and a *confrontation*. That it was also at times a *mingling* will be apparent to those who will have learned to detect that in the fields of religion and law,

---

[6] S. C. Franklin, "The Empire of the *Rhomaioi* as viewed from Kievan Russia: Aspects of Byzantino-Russian Cultural Relations", *Byzantion*, 53 (1983), p. 513.

literature and art the Orthodox peoples of Eastern Europe were able in the course of time not only to share in, but also to contribute to, the common culture of the Byzantine Commonwealth. It is worth recalling in this context the acute observation made in 1764 by the Scottish social thinker Adam Ferguson: "If nations actually borrow from their neighbors, they probably borrow only what they are nearly in a condition to have invented themselves."[7]

How far was the encounter between Byzantium and the Slavs, in Dupront's terms, "a trial of strength"? We must expect to find that Byzantine civilization, as it spread northward and westward to the Empire's neighbours, encountered some resistance. The social, moral and political values which it represented were often quite alien to the patterns of their own inherited culture. In the main, as far as we can judge from the sources, resistance took two distinct forms. In the early Middle Ages, the intrusive civilization of Byzantium was fought by the Slavs primarily on religious grounds: attempts were made to halt the advance of the Christian faith by resorting, in the name of the threatened pagan traditions, to passive resistance or armed insurrection; while the success enjoyed by the dualist Bogomil movement among the Balkan Slavs shows that Byzantine civilization could sometimes be withstood and repelled by the Slavs with the same weapons—the moral and theological teaching of Christianity—which the Byzantines used to extend their influence.[8] In the late Middle Ages the challenge to Byzantine hegemony became more overtly political. In several Slavic coun-

---

[7] A. Ferguson, "An Essay on the History of Civil Society", in *Readings in Early Anthropology*, ed. J. S. Slotkin (Chicago, 1965), p. 435.

[8] See "Le traité contre les Bogomiles de Cosmas le Prêtre", transl. H.-C. Puech and A. Vaillant (Paris, 1945); D. Obolensky, *The Bogomils* (Cambridge, 1948).

tries it took the form of sporadic efforts to impugn or question the claims of imperial power and of the church authorities of Constantinople to exercise by right a universal jurisdiction throughout Christendom. These manifestations of local nationalism remained on the whole in an embryonic state. Yet they are worth studying as examples of the strains and stresses which often developed in those East European societies which were subjected to prolonged cultural contact with the dominant Byzantine civilization. Such encounters were indeed, in Dupront's term, *"des rencontres-choc."*

The most interesting of these resistance movements are recorded in the early Middle Ages; and most of the evidence comes from Russian sources. The social picture is usually much the same: the forceful introduction of Byzantine patterns into the pagan societies of Eastern Europe creates an explosive situation, in which the accumulated anxieties provoked by the threat to the old ways of life erupts in sudden panic or despair. These anxieties can be observed in three successive stages in these societies' surrender to the impact of Byzantine civilization. At first this impact is perceived as a remote menace, as yet incapable of destroying the cherished tradition of the past: vigilance and occasional resort to social pressure are sufficient to keep it at bay. A situation of this kind seems to be implied in the words ascribed in the Russian chronicle in the tenth century to Prince Svyatoslav of Kiev, whom his mother, the saintly princess Olga, was trying to persuade to become a Christian: "How could I alone accept another religion? My retainers will laugh at me". The fear of ridicule in this case was a strong enough weapon in the hands of the prince's military retinue to enforce his conformity to the old pagan way of life.

In the second stage of the encounter between the old and the new order the situation is more critical. The invasion of the traditional culture has already taken place; the pagan cults and beliefs have been outlawed by the newly converted rulers, and an intensive campaign of reeducation has been started by the local authorities and their Byzantine advisers, with the avowed aim of replacing them by a new set of values: these could range over a large area of human conduct and belief, from Christian theology and marriage laws to details of dress and personal hygiene. At this point, when the old traditions, though in full retreat, still retain their appeal and the new imports have not yet been assimilated, the society is threatened with disaffection or schism. The adherents of the old culture, if unwilling to renounce it, can do one of two things: they can either stake their lives on a desperate bid to destroy the new order and its representatives; or sink into a state of passive despondency, in fruitless regret for bygone days. The leaders of the Old Bulgar clans, who soon after their ruler Boris' baptism in 864 and his decision to impose Greek Christianity on all his subjects tried to assassinate him and replace him by their own nominee, opted for the first solution. Boris' own account of this event shows that, in rising in defence of their cherished beliefs, privileges and customs, they rebelled not only against the Christian religion, but against the whole Byzantine fabric in which it had been forcibly imposed on their country.

An example of the second type of hostile reaction is found in the sequel to the Russian chronicler's story of how Prince Vladimir of Kiev, immediately after his conversion and the baptism of his subjects (about 990), had the children of the leading families of Rus' conscripted for education. He was not the first nor the last to realize that the building of a new social order and ideology requires a planned indoctrination of the young, and that this can best be achieved by removing them from the influence of their parents. The reaction of the pupils' families to these state schools was predictable. The Russian chronicler records with characteristic irony: "The mothers of these children wept over them, for they were not yet strong in the faith, and mourned for them, as though they were dead." The absence of any reference to the fathers' reactions may be due to the monastic chronicler's anti-feminine prejudice; yet it seems more likely that he was implying that the men-folk of the Russian aristocracy had already been won over to the new Christian order and supported their ruler's educational campaign. It is the women who appear in this story as the sorrowful and powerless representatives of family tradition and of the old dying culture.

The last stage in the confrontation between Byzantium and the pre-Christian culture of Eastern Europe leads us away from the limelight of royal courts and large cities, where the change is often rapid and dramatic, to the obscure and seemingly motionless life of remote village communities. The nation has now been officially Christian for several decades; its ruling and urban classes, the first to adopt the new faith, are striving to imitate, at least in their public life, their Byzantine mentors; court ceremonial and dress are modelled on those of Constantinople; public buildings, ecclesiastical and secular, are constructed on the Byzantine architectural pattern; artists and craftsmen from Constantinople and Thessalonica have been invited to decorate them; a tradition of literature and learning is growing in the cities; and very slowly, through the work of the missionaries and growing administrative centralization, this urban and aristocratic culture has begun to spread to the pagan countryside. There the immemorial customs, sacrificial offerings of food and animals, magical rites of fertility, the cult of fire and other natural elements, and the social prestige enjoyed by soothsayers and shamans, come under severe pressure from the invading culture. Ancient holy places and popular idols are profaned and overthrown, and Christian churches are built on the sites where they stood. Only in comparatively rare and harmless cases does the Christian clergy, native or Byzantine, show willingness to adapt pagan customs and beliefs to the imperious demands of the new religion. Resistance is either crushed or forestalled by the military power of the state. The resultant shock is so severe that these primitive communities, whose social life has been centred on the now proscribed customs and values, gradually sink into hopelessness. In such a case it needs but a further blow to their well-being, a famine, a drought, or the confiscation of their lands for the benefit of the church, to bring their frustration to a boiling point. And if at this juncture a prophet arises among them who promises to release them from their bondage and bring back the good old days by supernatural means, they will rally round him with the courage of despair.

Such revivalist movements were common among the Indian tribes of North America in the nineteenth century. Several striking instances of the same phenomenon were recorded in eleventh-century Rus'. The main centres of unrest were on the periphery of the land, the forest zone between the upper Volga and the Oka, and the remote "White Lake" region in the far north: frontier districts where the Eastern Slavs were intermingled with Finnic tribes. The story of these various revolts, as told by the Russian Primary Chronicle, followed a similar pattern. "Magicians" (*volkhvy* in Russian) of local peasant origin, operating in famine-stricken districts, persuaded their followers to massacre members of the landowning aristocracy on the grounds that they were hoarding food. Militantly anti-Christian (on one occasion they murdered a priest), they claimed secret knowledge, supernatural powers, and the gift of prophecy. The Russian authorities dealt ruthlessly with these shamans: in 1024 some were executed or banished; another group, who murdered wealthy women, were lynched by order of the prince of Kiev's tax collector (c. 1071).

These movements, pagan and peasant in character, were directed against the new religious and social order that was being imposed by the combined power of state and church. How dangerous they could be to both is shown by two episodes that occurred about 1071 and which show that these revivalist movements were not confined to the backward and rural districts of Rus'. One of these "magicians" came to Kiev, the capital of the land, where he rallied his supporters by prophesying that in four years' time the Dnieper would start to flow backwards and Byzantium and Russia would exchange places, "so that the Greek land would be where Rus' was, and Rus' where the Greek land was." For all the obscurity of this oracular utterance, it is not too fanciful to interpret it as a sign of the obsessive fear of Byzantium and all its works, which must have gripped the heart of more than one half-defeated pagan leader in eleventh-century Rus'. Another shaman appeared at that time in Novgorod, "pretending to be a god, and he led almost the entire city astray, claiming to foresee all things, reviling the Christian faith, and saying that he would walk across the Volkhov river, in the sight of all." The rebellion was finally quelled, but not before the entire population of the city, except the bishop, the prince and his retinue, had espoused the prophet's cause. The wholesale apostasy of the second most important city in Russia shows that the future of Byzantine Christianity was still far from assured nearly a hundred years after the country's official conversion.

These examples will have shown that the encounter between Byzantium and the natives of Eastern Europe could indeed become a "trial of strength." For Byzantine civilization, as it spread to the countries of Eastern Europe, met at times with a resistance that was sometimes widespread and powerful. Why then, we may ask, did these countries borrow so much and so readily from Byzantium? Political and economic, as well as cultural, reasons played a major role. Particular cultural traits were adopted because of their functional usefulness in solving a social problem or satisfying a material need: thus Christianity could help to overcome internal frictions due to ethnic diversity within the "receiving" country; the Byzantine doctrine of the divine origin of political authority sustained the local monarch's ambition to increase his power over his subjects; ability to tap the springs of Byzantine technological skill enabled him to carry out difficult engineering projects, such as the building of bridges and fortresses; while commercial and ecclesiastical links with the Empire satisfied the ruling classes' appetite for objects of luxury, impressive buildings, and education. The craving for beauty and learning and for the prestige attendant on their possession provided the strongest of incentives for the acquisition of Byzantine literature, law and art.

In the last resort, however, the factor which helped the most to overcome local resistance to Byzantine civilization was the unrivalled prestige which it came to enjoy throughout Eastern Europe. Until the twelfth century no other European country could hope to compete with the Byzantine empire, whether in wealth, power, or cultural achievements. To be associated with it was an eagerly sought honor.

Byzantine prestige was, of course, also closely linked with the appeal of the Christian religion. Modern historians tend to stress, and rightly so, the social and political motives which brought medieval rulers to the baptismal font. Yet we should not dismiss too lightly the interpretation placed on these events by contemporary chroniclers and hagiographers for whom the driving force of personal belief was the decisive factor. It would be rash to regard the conversion of Boris of Bulgaria, or of Olga and Vladimir of Rus' as no more than far-sighted acts of worldly statesmen, prompted by self-interest. What we know of their lives after baptism is at least compatible with the view that their conversions were genuine and that their Christian beliefs were held with sincerity. The precise nature and scope of these beliefs can hardly be determined, for lack of reliable evidence. In some cases the Gospel teaching, with its message of spiritual and moral regeneration, must have had a real impact. At other times the beauty of liturgical worship, perceived through eye and ear, softened and held captive the hearts of men and women. And within the ruling societies of Eastern Europe, whose religious and social preoccupations had centered hitherto on family, clan, tribe or kingdom, there must have been not a few to whom the universal perspective of the Christian religion offered a novel and deeply appealing experience.[9]

If on the higher levels of society, the East European peoples looked to the Byzantines as their mentors in matters of doctrine, the attitude of the simpler folk was more instinctive and spontaneous. It found striking expression in the reverence for the city of Constantinople, which in their language the Slavs called *Tsargrad*, the imperial city. For the whole of Eastern Christendom Constantinople was a holy city, not only because it was the seat of the emperor and of his spiritual partner, the oecumenical patriarch. Its principal claim to holiness lay in the supernatural forces believed to be present within its walls: the memorials of Christ's passion and the many relics of saints; the

---

[9] Cf. D. Obolensky, *The Byzantine Commonwealth* (London, 1971), pp. 283–9, parts of which are repeated in the previous few pages.

churches and monasteries, repositories of prayer and famed shrines of Christendom; above all, the patronage of its heavenly protectors, the Divine Wisdom, whose temple was St. Sophia, and the Theotokos, whose robe, preserved in the Church of Blachernae, was venerated as the city's palladium.

In the aura of sanctity which surrounded it, Constantinople was often thought of as the New Jerusalem, its only rival. The East European pilgrims and travellers who visited Constantinople in the Middle Ages displayed before the number of its relics and the holiness of its sanctuaries the same open-eyed wonder and religious awe which they reveal in their descriptions of the Holy Land. More than one of them dwells on the breath-taking beauty of the Great Church of St. Sophia and on the loveliness of its liturgical chanting: "a chant", declared Antony, the future archbishop of Novgorod who visited the city in the year 1200, "like that of the angels." In his and other accounts which medieval Russian pilgrims have left us, we sometimes catch an echo of the same excitement with which the envoys of Vladimir of Rus' are said to have reported to their sovereign their impressions of the public worship in Constantinople: "We knew not whether we were in heaven or on earth." For the nations of the Byzantine Commonwealth Constantinople was not only "the eye of the world" (*opthalmos tis oikoumenes*), but also "the city of the world's desire" (*he kosmopampothetos polis*). Thus in the "trial of strength" which, as we have seen, so often marked the process of acculturation, Byzantium was often, in the last resort, victorious.

During another international congress of historical studies, the sixteenth, held in Stuttgart in 1985, the process of acculturation was given a further, and perhaps more subtle, dimension. One of the congress's principal themes was entitled "The Image of the Other" (*L'Image de l'Autre*). The author of one of the papers presented in this section, Michel Mollat du Jourdain, drew an arresting contrast between the egocentric projection on to the Other of a counter-image of Self, and the readiness to accept the Other on his own terms. I quote from his paper, in a translation from the French:

> When one is willing to consider the Other for himself and in himself, to understand him and in a sense to forget oneself, to acknowledge that one is not every-thing and does not know everything, that the Other can know other things, at that moment dialogue be-comes possible, and the images become authentic.[10]

Viewed in this light, the dialogue implicit in the act of acculturation acquires a spiritual dimension. Its ultimate goal, one of identification, lies no doubt beyond the power of soci-eties and most individuals to achieve. But it can perhaps be illustrated poetically by a Tibetan parable, cited by Metropoli-tan Anthony of Sourozh in one of his books on prayer:

A doll of salt, after a long journey on dry land, came to the sea, and discovered something she had never seen and could not understand. She stood there on firm ground, a solid little doll of salt, and saw that there was another ground that was mobile, insecure, noisy, strange and unknown. So she asked the sea: "What are you?" And it said: "I am the sea". And the doll said: "What is the sea?" To which the answer was: "It is I". Then the doll said: "I cannot understand, but I want to; how can I?" The sea answered: "Touch me". So the doll shyly put forward a foot, and touched the water, and she got a strange impression that it was something that began to be knowable. She withdrew her leg, looked, and saw that her toes had gone,

---

[10] "L'image de l'Autre dans la mentalité occidentale à la fin du Moyen Age", in *Rapports du XVIe Congrès international des sciences historiques*, I (Stuttgart, 1985), p. 105.

and she was afraid, and said: "Oh, but where is my toe, and what have you done to me?" And the sea said: "You have given something in order to understand." Gradually the water took away small bits of the doll's salt, and the doll went further and further into the sea, and at every moment she had a sense of understanding more and more, yet she was not able to say what the sea was. As she went deeper, she melted more and more, repeating: "But what is the sea?" At last a wave dissolved the rest of her, and the doll cried out: "It is I."[11]

THE CYRILLO-METHODIAN TRADITION

In my last lecture I discussed the term "acculturation"; and I hope to have shown that this concept can usefully be applied to the impact of Byzantium upon the medieval Slav countries— to the study, in other words, of the Byzantine-Slavic dialogue. I will begin today's lecture by making a further general point. In addition to those basic features of acculturation of which I spoke last time—movement, education, mingling, and confrontation—one further element, I believe, should be added to the equation to ensure its success. To be really fruitful, the Byzantine-Slav encounter required more than imperial diplomacy and missionary zeal, or a simple East European quest for culture. It had to take place, I believe, in an ambience common to both worlds and capable of acting in relation to them, as an intermediary or catalyst. This ambience, in turn needed to pos-

[11] Metropolitan Anthony (Archbishop Anthony Bloom), *Living Prayer* (London, 1966), pp. 105–6. Cf. St. Catherine of Genoa (1447–1510): "My Me is God, nor do I recognise any other Me, except my God Himself". Cited in F. von Hügel, *The Mystical Element of Religion as studied in Saint Catherine of Genoa and her Friends*, vol. I (London, 1908), p. 265. I am indebted for this reference to Bishop Kallistos (Timothy) Ware.

sess three essential qualities: a creative energy powerful enough to leave its mark on religious beliefs, literary values, and social and political ideas; a cosmopolitan character, giving it power to cross state boundaries and linguistic frontiers and to be seen as a common East European tradition; and it would have to attract and retain the loyalties of men of different nations, linking them by common discipleship and the ties of friendship.

In the medieval period with which these lectures are concerned, Byzantium and the Slavic world came to be linked by effective cultural intermediaries on two occasions: the first time in the early Middle Ages, in the ninth, tenth, and eleventh centuries; and again in the century between 1350 and 1450. Each of these occasions saw the rise and spread of a vigorous cultural tradition: each of them has provided the title for my two remaining lectures. Today we shall be concerned with the Cyrillo-Methodian tradition. Its linguistic idiom—the Old Church Slavonic language—at once modeled on Greek and close to the Slav vernacular tongues, provided the Slavs with a channel ensuring a regular flow of influence from the Byzantine world, enabling them to develop a culture that was Greek in content and Slav in form. As we shall see, it provided the peoples of Eastern Europe, at the time of their conversion to Christianity, with an instrument of great cultural potency which enabled them to build up fairly rapidly a literary tradition based on Byzantine models.

The Hesychast tradition, the subject of my third lecture, proved an equally powerful catalyst. Monastic in origin, spearheaded by the hermitages of Mount Athos and the Patriarchate of Constantinople, fostered locally by a confraternity of devoted Slav and Roumanian monks, and overflowing into literature and perhaps into art, this movement linked together, more closely than ever before, the different parts of the Byzantine cultural commonwealth. Its intermediary role between the Greek and the Slav worlds proved, as we shall see, no less important than that played by the Cyrillo-Methodian tradition three or four centuries earlier.

So, today, our subject is the Cyrillo-Methodian tradition. It takes its name from two Byzantine missionaries who, in the ninth century, strove to build, in the heart of Central Europe, a Slavic vernacular church under the joint auspices of Byzantium and Rome. They were the two brothers, Constantine and Methodius. Constantine is better known under his later monastic name of Cyril: hence the adjective Cyrillo-Methodian. They were natives of Salonica (Thessaloniki), after Constantinople the most important city in the Byzantine Empire. In so far as this term can be meaningfully applied to ninth-century Byzantines, they were in my opinion Greeks; and the efforts of some historians to prove that they were wholly or partly Slav by birth seem to me misguided.[12] They came from a family with a tradition of public service. Methodius, the elder, held for a while a high administrative post in one of the Slav provinces of the Empire. Constantine was given an extensive education in Constantinople during the 840s. He is said to have studied at the feet of the two leading scholars of his age, Leo the Mathematician and Photius, the future patriarch. He was certainly a protégé of the Logothete Theoktistos, the chief statesman of the Empire. Both brothers experienced an early call to the religious life. Methodius became a monk in the great monastic foundation of Mount Olympus in western Asia Minor; Constantine, who for the time being remained in the Byzantine capital, was ordained deacon or priest (which of

[12] See A.-E. Tachiaos, "L'origine de Cyrille et de Méthode. Verité et légende dans les sources slaves", *Cyrillomethodianum*, II (1972–1973), pp. 98–140; I. Sevcenko, "On the Social Background of Cyril and Methodius", *Studia Palaeoslovenica*, 1971, pp. 341–51.

the two we do not know for certain) and was appointed to a chair in the University of Constantinople.

Most of our knowledge of their lives comes from their two Slavic biographies, known to scholars today as the *Vita Constantini* and the *Vita Methodii*.[13] We know today that the *Vita Constantini* was written within thirteen years of Constantine-Cyril's death; and that the *Vita Methodii* was composed soon after Methodius' death in 885. They are thus to all intents and purposes contemporary biographies. Their authenticity and reliability were demonstrated in an important book published in Prague in 1933. Its author, Father Dvornik, my teacher, was able to show how accurately they reflect the intellectual climate and culture of ninth-century Byzantium.[14] An English translation of both texts was published in 1976 by the University of Michigan.[15]

To assess the role played by the Cyrillo-Methodian tradition as an intermediary in the Byzantine-Slavic dialogue, we must first, briefly, look at the history of the mission of these two brothers to the Slavs. The story begins in 862. In that year an embassy arrived in Constantinople, sent to the Emperor Michael III by a Slav ruler in Central Europe, the Moravian prince Rastislav. The purpose of this embassy seems to have been twofold: the Moravians, whose realm comprised what is today the Czech republic, Slovakia, and western Hungary, were hard pressed by their neighbours, the Franks and the Bulgarians, and probably wished to conclude a political alliance with Byzantium. The second aim of the embassy was destined to

[13] Constantinus et Methodius Thessalonicenses, *Fontes*, ed. F. Grivec and F. Tomsic (Zagreb, 1960).
[14] F. Dvornik, *Les légendes de Constantin et de Méthode vues de Byzance* (Prague, 1933; Hattiesburg, Miss., 1969).
[15] Transl. M. Kantor and R. S. White: *Michigan Slavic Materials*, no. 13, 1976.

be, in the long run, of far greater importance. It was to request the Emperor to send the Moravians a Christian missionary acquainted with the Slavic language. Christianity had already spread to Moravia during the first half of the ninth century, but its preachers were German missionaries from Salzburg and Passau. Rastislav feared that they would threaten the precarious and indeed ephemeral independence he had recently wrested from his overlord Louis the German, King of Bavaria. A Slav-speaking clergy from Byzantium, he hoped, would help him safeguard his country's cultural independence.

Constantine and Methodius were the obvious choice to lead the Byzantine embassy to Moravia. Distinguished in the service of church and state, experienced diplomats, they had the added advantage of knowing the Slavic language. Salonica, their native town, was in the ninth century a bilingual city, with a Slav speaking countryside around. Methodius' biographer tells us that the emperor, in urging him and his brother to go to Moravia, adduced the following argument: "You are both natives of Thessaloniki, and all Thessalonians speak pure Slav."[16]

Before leaving Constantinople, Constantine invented an alphabet for the use of the Moravian Slavs. This invention was not instantaneous; and we know that he had collaborators who—perhaps over several years—had helped him in his task: chief among them was his brother Methodius. Constantine's alphabet—known today as Glagolitic—was adapted to a Slav dialect of southern Macedonia, from the neighbourhood of Salonica. With the help of his new alphabet, before leaving Constantinople, he translated a selection of lessons from the Gospels, intended for liturgical use. According to this *Vita*, he began with the opening words of St. John's Gospel, which in

---

[16] *Vita Methodii*, v, 8: Grivec and Tomsic, p. 155.

the Orthodox Church are read during the Easter liturgy: "In the beginning was the Word, and the Word was with God, and the Word was God."[17] Their symbolic relevance to the task of evangelizing the Slavs in their own language was surely lost neither on Constantine nor on his medieval biographer.

The Byzantine mission probably arrived in Moravia in the autumn of 863. Constantine, we are told by his biographer, rapidly translated the Greek liturgical offices into the Slav language. Thus was created a new literary language, based on the spoken dialect of the Macedonian Slavs. It is known to modern scholars as Old Church Slavonic. Because the different Slavic languages were still very similar in structure and vocabulary, Old Church Slavonic was intelligible to all the Slavs. Yet Constantine, while safeguarding the essential qualities of the Slavonic vocabulary and syntax, was able to enrich the new language with loan words, semantic calques and stylistic devices borrowed from the Greek. The imprint of the Greek language upon Old Church Slavonic, and thus upon the literature of medieval Eastern Europe, proved indelible. In the course of time the range of Old Church Slavonic was broadened and its vocabulary enriched by further translations of the Christian scripture, of Greek patristic writings and of Byzantine legal texts, as well as by original works. Old Church Slavonic became, after Greek and Latin, the third international language of Europe and the common literary idiom of those East European peoples—the Bulgarians, the Serbs, the Ukrainians, the Russians and the Roumanians—who gained entry into the Byzantine cultural commonwealth. Constantine, with his brother Methodius, was thus the founder of a cultural tradition, Greek in form and Slavic in content, which was to provide

---

[17] *Vita Constantini*, xiv, 14: Grivec and Tomsic, p. 129.

a channel of great efficacy for the transmission of Byzantine culture to the medieval peoples of Eastern Europe.

It was of great importance to the history of the Cyrillo-Methodian mission that it was carried out in an atmosphere of intense struggle. The two brothers, as well as their leading disciples, became perforce fighters: fighters for a cause that had to be defended by sustained and powerful argument. They had come to Moravia at the express request of that country's authorities: but Moravia belonged to Western Christendom, and to this land the Byzantines could lay no convincing claim. Two further difficulties stood in the way of the mission. The Frankish clergy, who had worked in Moravia for the past half-century, regarded these upstart missionaries, not without reason, as trespassers on their own missionary preserve. Furthermore, these Greeks from Byzantium were engaged in a liturgical and linguistic experiment which seemed to the Franks a suspect, indeed heretical, novelty: they celebrated the divine office not in Latin, as the custom of the Western Church commanded, but in Slavic. And so, from the very onset of their mission, Constantine and Methodius were plagued by Frankish suspicion and hostility.

There was only one European power capable of supporting effectively the Cyrillo-Methodian mission: this was the Papacy, in whose overall jurisdiction Moravia lay. Four years after their arrival in that country, Constantine and Methodius travelled to Rome, in response to a summons from Pope Nicholas I. To understand the events that followed, we must bear in mind one essential fact: in the ninth century, and indeed for some considerable time to come, the Greek and the Roman Churches, despite growing rivalry and doctrinal and liturgical disputes, were still a single body: a consciousness of a united Christendom had as yet forsaken neither: for most Byzantines of the time, Rome remained the venerable city of Peter and

Paul, and in its bishop, the Patriarch of the West—the "Apostolicus" as he is called in the *Vita Constantini* and the *Vita Methodii*—was vested the primacy of honour in the whole of Christendom. It is important to recognize that the attitude of Constantine and Methodius to Rome and its bishop in no way differed from that of most of their Byzantine compatriots.

In Rome they were warmly received by the new pope, Hadrian II. The pope, in a decision that broke for a while the liturgical monopoly of Latin in the Western Church, solemnly authorized the use of the Slavonic liturgy.

At this crucial moment in the mission's history, Constantine fell seriously ill. Feeling the approach of death, he became a monk under his now more familiar name of Cyril. In 869 he died in Rome and, at his brother's request, was buried in the Church of San Clemente. His last words to his brother were to beg him not to abandon their common work for the Slavs, even if it meant never returning to the monastery of Mount Olympus, where Methodius had received the tonsure. This injunction, recorded by Methodius' ninth-century biographer, provides a moving illustration of the tension we find so often in the history of the Church between the missionary calling and the contemplative life: "Behold, my brother, we were both harnessed to the same yoke, ploughing the same furrow. I am falling down on the field, my day's work finished; but you have a great love of the Mountain. Do not, for the sake of the Mountain, abandon your teaching. For how better can you be saved?"[18]

The rest of Methodius' life was spent in obedience to his brother's last wish. Armed with the pope's approval of the Slavic liturgy, he returned to Central Europe where, as archbishop of Pannonia and papal legate to the Slav nations, he continued the work of building a vernacular Christianity, translating the

---

[18] *Vita Methodii*, vii, 1–3: Grivec and Tomsic, p. 157.

remaining parts of the Scriptures and training the next generation of Slav-speaking priests. But the East Frankish clergy, whose prerogatives in Central Europe had been annulled by Methodius' appointment, struck again. Taking advantage of the dethronement of Rastislav of Moravia by his nephew, who promptly acknowledged the suzerainty of Louis the German, they secured Methodius' arrest. For two and a half years Methodius was imprisoned in Germany. Only in 873 did the new pope, John VIII, learning at last of his legate's plight, force Louis the German and the Bavarian bishops to release and reinstate him.

But Rome was fast losing interest in the Slavic liturgy. The Papacy, it seems, was now showing an increasing unwillingness to risk, for the sake of this liturgy, a major conflict with the Frankish church. John VIII still loyally supported Methodius. But his successors, turning their back on the policy of Nicholas I and Hadrian II, banned the Slavic liturgy. In 885 Methodius died in Moravia, his work among the Slavs on the brink of ruin. His principal disciples were arrested and exiled from Moravia; others were sold into slavery.

The later history of the Cyrillo-Methodian mission lies outside the scope of this lecture. We should note, however, that at the very moment when the work of the two brothers in Central Europe seemed to have utterly collapsed, a promising future suddenly opened before it. Expelled from Moravia on their master's death, the disciples of Methodius found refuge in another land. Their work was saved for Europe and the Slavs by the Bulgarians, who further enriched this vernacular tradition and, in the fullness of time, transmitted it to the other peoples of Eastern Europe who belonged to the Byzantine cultural commonwealth. Clement, the chief disciple of Cyril and Methodius, after his expulsion from Moravia, worked among the Macedonian Slavs for thirty years. He and his companion Naum continued their masters' work in Bulgaria in the late ninth century, preaching in the Slav language, celebrating the Slavic liturgy according to the Byzantine rite, translating Greek religious writings with the help of the newly invented Cyrillic alphabet, and training a native clergy. And here this all too brief outline of the mission's history must, for our present purpose, end.

I now come to the second part of my paper. I will now invite you to reflect on several features of the Cyrillo-Methodian tradition. Especially on its role as a factor of unity and an intermediary in the encounter, or the dialogue, between Byzantium and the Slavs.

The role was assured, in the first place, by its supranational character. In opening up the religious and cultural world of Byzantium to the peoples of Eastern Europe, Old Church Slavonic enabled them to make their own distinctive contribution to that world. The writings in that language, composed before 1100 in Moravia, Bohemia, Croatia, Bulgaria and Rus', are now increasingly regarded as creations of a single, supra-national, literature. The nationalistic point of view of earlier literary historians, who tended to treat works written in ninth-century Macedonia, tenth century Bohemia, and eleventh-century Kiev as products of separate Bulgarian, Czech, and Russian literatures, though still entrenched in textbooks, is—I believe—being gradually abandoned today. However, the history of this common literature has yet to be written, and until we have a detailed comparative study of its principal works all conclusions regarding it must remain tentative. We do know, however, that cultural intercourse between the different parts of the Byzantine Commonwealth was promoted by a brisk circulation of Old Church Slavonic manuscripts. From Moravia,

Cyrillo-Methodian writings were carried to Bohemia, Croatia, and Bulgaria; from Bulgaria to Rus'; the Russians also borrowed and absorbed into their own literature works produced in Moravia and Bohemia.

These migrations of texts, formerly thought to result from successive waves of reciprocal national "influences," are now seen rather as the circulation within a single international community of one body of literature regarded as its common heritage. Two distinguished scholars have recently pioneered this change of emphasis: Roman Jakobson and Dmitri Sergeevich Likhachev. The latter developed the now influential concept of "intermediary literature" (*literatura-posrednitsa*) which he defined as a "literature which creates a special fund of texts, and exists simultaneously on the national territories of a number of countries as a single developing whole."[19] An example of this new thinking is Boris Uspensky's recent study (1983) of "the Church-Slavonic/Russian *diglossia*," which leads him to postulate "a single Helleno-Slavic language which manifests itself either as Greek, or as Church Slavonic."[20] And the same idea was put forward earlier by Alexander Isachenko, who defined Old Church Slavonic as "the Greek language, clothed in Slavic (Bulgarian) morphemes."[21]

Another feature of the Cyrillo-Methodian tradition worth mentioning in this context is the use its leading representatives made of what may be called "ethnic self-determination." They believed that, by acquiring the Scriptures and the Liturgy in

[19] D. S. Likhachev, *Razvitie russkoy literatury X–XVII vekov,* (Leningrad, 1973), p. 24.

[20] B. A. Uspensky, *Yazykovaya situatsiya Kievskoy Rusi i ee znachenie dlya istorii russkogo literaturnogo yazyka* [IX Mezhdunarodnyi s'ezd slavistov: Doklady] (Moscow, 1983), p. 21.

[21] See A. Isachenko, in *Russian Linguistics*, I (1974), p. 340; idem, *Geschichte der russischen Sprache*, I (Heidelberg, 1980), p. 81.

their own language, the Slavs entered a privileged society: a society in which every nation has its own peculiar gifts and every people its legitimate calling. Their language had now acquired a sacramental character; and the nation which spoke it was, in its turn, held to be raised to the status of a "peculiar," consecrated people. Here, you see, the idea of a consecrated nation is combined with that of a plurality of languages equal in status, and the incipient nationalism of the countries of Eastern Europe was tempered and sublimated by what would be called today an ecumenical outlook. A joyful optimism seems to bring to many of the early writings of the Cyrillo-Methodian tradition the breath of a cultural springtime; it comes from the Slavs' awareness that, by receiving the Christian "letters" in their own language, they have acquired a distinct historical identity. To have entered this elitist society must have been a heady experience. The Emperor Michael, in a letter written to the Moravian ruler which he probably entrusted to Cyril and Methodius before they left Constantinople, wrote, with reference to the newly invented Slavonic Liturgy: "Accept a gift greater and more precious than gold or silver or precious stones or transient riches … so that you also may be numbered among the great nations which render glory to God in their own language".[22]

It is, I think, worth noting that this Cyrillo-Methodian concept of spiritual self-determination was repeatedly emphasized by the present Pope, in his Encyclical Epistle *Slavorum Apostoli*, issued in 1985 to commemorate the eleven-hundredth anniversary of the death of St. Methodius. John Paul II, who five years earlier had proclaimed Sts. Cyril and Methodius Co-Patrons of Europe, now cited, in illustration of the apostolic nature of their work, these words from the Second Vatican

[22] *Vita Constantini*, xiv, 16, 18: Grivec and Tomsic, p. 129.

Council's Dogmatic Constitution of the Church: "This characteristic of universality which adorns the People of God is a gift from the Lord himself. … In virtue of this catholicity each individual part of the Church contributes through its special gifts to the good of the other parts and of the whole Church. Thus through the common sharing of gifts and through the common effort to attain fullness in unity, the whole and each of its parts receive increase."[23]

I mentioned earlier that the Cyrillo-Methodian mission was carried out, at least in its earliest phase, in an atmosphere of intense struggle. Cyril and Methodius and their immediate disciples had to defend the new Slavic liturgy from the attacks of its enemies. Its first recorded opponents were, you will recall, the Frankish clerics in Central Europe. A little later, in Venice, on their way to Rome, the two brothers met with fiercer and, it seems, more articulate opposition from local Latin bishops and priests. Constantine was forced to refute their central argument, that it is permissible to celebrate the divine office only in three languages—Hebrew, Greek, and Latin—a view he condemned as the "trilingual heresy." Against this doctrine, widespread in the West and, it seems, not quite unknown in Eastern Christendom, Cyril and Methodius and their disciples were to fight their hardest verbal battles. *Vita Constantini*, chapter 16, the source of our knowledge of this episode, using the vocabulary of epic poetry, states that the Latin bishops, priests and monks gathered against him in Venice "like ravens against a falcon."[24] Constantine met their attacks with two arguments; the first was drawn from historical precedent, the second from

---

[23] John Paul II, Encyclical Epistle *Slavorum Apostoli* (Vatican City, 1985), p. 29. I am indebted for the knowledge of this text to Mgr. Bryan Chestle.
[24] *Vita Constantini*, xvi, i: Grivec and Tomsic, p. 134.

Scripture. He cited a list of peoples who, in his words, "give glory to God each in its own language." This list, some of whose items still cause headaches to scholars, includes Armenians, Georgians, Persians, Goths and Arabs. But the heaviest artillery Constantine moved against the Venetian trilingualists was his citation of virtually the entire fourteenth chapter of St. Paul's First Epistle to the Corinthians. Here are some telling passages:

> If the trumpet give an uncertain sound, who shall prepare himself to the battle? So likewise ye, except ye utter by the tongue words easy to be understood, how shall it be known what is spoken? For ye shall speak into the air. … For if I pray in an unknown tongue, my spirit prayeth, but my understanding is unfruitful. … Yet in the church I had rather speak five words with my understanding, that by my voice I might teach others also, than ten thousand words in an unknown tongue.[25]

It matters little, for our present purpose, that Constantine and his medieval biographer were quoting St. Paul out of context, and that I Corinthians 14 has nothing whatever to do with vernacular languages. What St. Paul is in fact saying is that "speaking in tongues," that is making ecstatic utterance, is less useful to the Christian community than rational and coherent preaching. It remains true, however, that I Corinthians 14, with its strong emphasis on intelligibility must have become an ideological manifesto for more than one writer of the Cyrillo-Methodian school.

Thus, in the last resort, the Cyrillo-Methodian apologetic literature finds its *raison d'être*, and its unifying role in the Byzantine cultural commonwealth, within the tradition of Christian

---

[25] *Vita Constantini*, xvi, 21: Grivec and Tomsic, pp. 135–6.

Scripture. I would like, in conclusion, to cite a few examples of the richness and variety of this apologetic tradition.

The *Vita Methodii* cites, in an adapted Slavic translation, the letter written in 869 by Pope Hadrian II to the Slav princes of Central Europe.[26] In this letter, which begins with the words "Glory to God in the highest, on earth peace, good-will toward men" the Pope announces the appointment of Methodius as his legate, and authorizes the use of the Slavic liturgy in the lands of these princes. And he adds, as justification for his action: "that the word of the Scriptures might be fulfilled"; "Praise the Lord, all ye nations," and: "All the different tongues shall tell the mighty works of God, as the Holy Spirit will give them utterance." The second of these quotations is taken, almost verbatim, from the second chapter of the Acts of the Apostles, verses 4 and 11, which describe the descent of tongues "like as of fire" upon the apostles at Pentecost. This shows that the Pope and the author of the *Vita Methodii* believed that the advent of the Slavic liturgy and of vernacular Scriptures was equivalent to a second Pentecost. The same parallel is drawn, at least implicitly, in other works of the Cyrillo-Methodian tradition.

This Pentecostal theme, applied to the Slav vernacular, acquires, in another work of the Cyrillo-Methodian tradition, a still broader dimension. The Russian Primary Chronicle, in an early section concerned with the Cyrillo-Methodian mission, repeats the same Pentecostal text from Acts 2 cited in the *Vita Methodii*. But the context in which it is placed is new. It forms part of the story, based on the Book of Genesis, which relates the division of the earth among the sons of Noah after the Flood, and the building of the Tower of Babel. The Russian chronicler goes on to say that when the Lord scattered

26 *Vita Methodii*, viii, 5, 13: Grivec and Tomsic, pp. 157–8.

His people over the face of the earth, the pristine unity of mankind gave way to a multiplicity of language and nations.[27] It is, I think, clear from the context of this passage that he wished to suggest a contrast between the former multiplicity of tongues and the present unity of the Slavic languages, a unity enhanced by the work of Cyril and Methodius; and that he did so by implying that the Slav vernacular writings are an extension of the miracle of Pentecost, whereby the Holy Spirit abolished the confusion of tongues which sprang from the Tower of Babel.

The idea that the Pentecostal miracle, by reuniting the languages of the earth, repealed the confusion of tongues which followed the building of the Tower of Babel, is a fairly common patristic theme. More immediately, and perhaps for the Russian chronicler more relevantly, it is repeatedly emphasized in the Byzantine offices for Whitsunday, or Pentecost. The *Kondakion* of the feast forcibly makes this point: "When the Most High went down and confused the tongues, He divided the nations; but when He distributed the tongues of fire, He called all men to unity."[28] The notion that the Slav peoples share in the Pentecostal abrogation of Babel can be regarded as a significant addition to the storehouse of Cyrillo-Methodian ideas.

The belief that the vernacular Christianity, created by Cyril and Methodius, has its place in the economy of human salvation, could be taken yet a step further. This step was taken by several medieval authors who saw in the Cyrillo-Methodian

---

[27] *Povest' vremennykh let*, ed. D. S. Likhachev, I (Moscow-Leningrad, 1950), pp. 9–10; English transl.: *The Russian Primary Chronicle* by S. H. Cross and O. P. Sherbowitz-Wetzor (Cambridge, Mass, n.d.), pp. 51–2

[28] *Ote katabas tas glossas synechee, diemerisen ethne ho Hypistosote tou pyros tas glossas dieveimen, eis enotita pantas ekalese: Pentekostarion Charmosynon* (Rome, 1883), p. 400.

heritage a portent of the transfiguration of the world through the advent of the Kingdom of God. And in this claim, however extravagant it may sound when put in these general terms, lies my final example.

Something of the kind seems to be implied in an Old Church Slavonic poem of the ninth century, the *Prologue (Proglas)* to the translated Gospels. Its theme is the apotheosis of vernacular writing, and the sacred right of the Slavs—indeed of all peoples—to possess the Scriptures in their own language. The late Roman Jakobson, the leading authority of our time on the Cyrillo-Methodian tradition, ascribed the *Prologue* to Constantine-Cyril himself, and called it "an unmatched classic of Slavic homiletic poetry." The author of the poem laments the fate of those without sacred books in their own language, and suggests that the Word, the *logos* the Slavs are now able to hear, can transfigure man's every sense. Here is Jakobson's translation of the passage:

> As without light there can be no joy—
> For while the eye sees all of God's creation,
> Still what is seen without light lacks beauty—
> So it is with every soul lacking letters,
> And ignorant even of God's law …
> The law that reveals God's paradise.
> For what ear, having heard
> The sound of thunder, is not gripped with the fear of
> God?
> Or how can nostrils which smell no flower
> Sense the divine miracle?
> And the mouth which tastes no sweetness
> Makes of man a stone.
> Even more, the soul lacking letters
> Grows dead in human beings.[29]

[29] R. Jakobson, *Selected Writings*, VI, 1 (Berlin-New York-Amsterdam, 1985), pp. 194–6

The sense of triumph and joy in the newly acquired Slavonic letters, which touch so many early medieval writings of the Cyrillo-Methodian school with the excitement of a cultural springtime, are conveyed most powerfully in another Biblical text from which the authors of the *Prologue*, of the *Vita Constantini*, and of the Russian Primary Chronicle quoted to describe the bounty of the Slav vernacular tradition. This text is found in the opening verses of the 35th chapter of the Book of the Prophet Isaiah, in the Septuagint version. It reads as follows:

> The wilderness and the dry land shall be glad, the desert shall rejoice and blossom; like the crocus it shall blossom abundantly, and rejoice with joy and singing. ... Then the eyes of the blind shall be opened, and the ears of the deaf shall be unstopped. Then shall the lame man leap like a hart, and the tongue of the dumb shall be clearly heard. ... They shall see the glory of the Lord, the splendour of our God.

THE HESYCHAST TRADITION

Last week I spoke of the Cyrillo-Methodian tradition. We looked at the role played by this movement as a cultural intermediary between Byzantium and the Slavs: as such an instrument of great power and appeal which enabled the Orthodox Slavs to develop, within their respective countries, a culture that was Greek in content and Slavic in form. The effectiveness of this bilingual tradition as an intermediary was, we saw, assured by three qualities which it possessed to a high degree: a creative energy which left its mark on religious beliefs, literature, and social and political ideas; a cosmopolitan character, enabling it to cross state boundaries and linguistic frontiers; and the ability to command the loyalties of an international group of men, linked by common discipleship and the ties of friendship.

Today's lecture—my third and last of the series—is concerned with a phenomenon which, though it began as a coherent movement several centuries later than the Cyrillo-Methodian one, proved equally important as a Byzantine-Slav intermediary; and, as we shall see, it shared with the Cyrillo-Methodian tradition the three qualities of spirituality, cosmopolitanism, and international sponsorship. This late medieval movement is known as Hesychasm.

A note of warning should be sounded here. The term "Hesychasm" has been used by scholars in a variety of meanings, some of which overlap. These semantic shifts have had a confusing effect on many students of history, theology, and art, who have used this term. In an endeavor to bring some order and clarity into this confusion, the late John Meyendorff distinguished four different meanings of the word "Hesychasm." (1) As a technical term borrowed from the vocabulary of the spiritual life, it can be applied, in the Greek term *hesychia* (from which it is derived) to the "prayer of the mind" (*noera proseuche*), or "prayer of the heart," practised by the early Christian hermits in Egypt, Palestine, and Asia Minor. (2) Modern writers sometimes apply the term "Hesychasm" to the psychosomatic "method," accompanying the frequent repetition of the "Jesus prayer," and designed to aid spiritual concentration. First clearly attested on Mount Athos in the late thirteenth century, the "Method" was widely used in Eastern Christian monasticism in the late Middle Ages. (3) Hesychasm is also taken to denote the theology of St. Gregory Palamas, Archbishop of Thessalonica in the fourteenth century. (4) The term has sometimes been applied to the cultural, social, and political programme devised and carried out by a succession of Byzantine Patriarchs who belonged to the Hesychast movement. This programme did much to strengthen the bonds between the Slav and Roumanian Orthodox Churches on the one hand and the Byzantine Patriarchate on the other in the late Middle Ages, and thus to cement the cultural unity of the Byzantine Commonwealth.[30]

In considering Hesychasm as a factor in the process of acculturation in late medieval Eastern Europe, and notably as a cultural intermediary between Byzantium and the Slav world, I will endeavor to show that the motive force that gave Hesychasm its spiritual content came from the principal monasteries of the Balkans, above all from Mount Athos; that the ecclesiastical policy which sustained Hesychasm and ensured its influence as an international movement originated in Constantinople; that the impact of Byzantine Hesychasm upon late medieval literature—especially in the field of hagiography—was particularly powerful in the Slav Orthodox countries, and also in Roumania; and that the cosmopolitan nature of the Hesychast movement was enhanced by the action of a group of men, most of them of outstanding ability and achievement, who had close personal links with each other and, frequently crossing national boundaries, freely moved from one part of the Byzantine Commonwealth to another.

First, then, monastic spirituality. In its original, technical, meaning the terms goes back to the early days of Eastern Christian monasticism in the fourth century, when hermits, living in solitude, or silence (*hesychia*) were called Hesychasts, partly to distinguish them from monks living in community. In this sense

---

[30] J. Meyendorff, "O vizantiyskom isikhazme i ego roli v kul'turnom i istoricheskom razvitii vostochnoy Evropy v XIV veke", *Trudy Otdela Drevnerusskoy Literatury*, 29 (1974), pp. 291–305.

hesychia is sometimes translated as "quietude," though a better rendering, proposed by Bishop Kallistos of Diokleia, is "inner stillness."[31] Gradually, and certainly by the thirteenth century, the "prayer of the heart" became linked with the frequent, and regular, repetition of the "Jesus prayer" ("Lord Jesus Christ, Son of God, have mercy upon me"), still much practised in the Orthodox Church, and with certain bodily exercises (such as the regulation of breathing), designed to aid spiritual concentration. Parallels have been suggested between these bodily techniques and certain Hindu and Muslim practices, though, as Bishop Kallistos rightly stresses, "the points of similarity must not be pressed too far."[32] It seems significant, however, that we have evidence showing that Byzantine monks in the thirteenth and fourteenth centuries were interested in the methods of prayer practised by the Brahmins of India.[33]

Mount Athos, with its group of monasteries on a mountainous peninsula in northern Greece, was, we have seen, a spiritual nursery of the Hesychast movement. Many of the movement's leaders, including Gregory of Sinai, Gregory Palamas, and the Patriarchs Kallistos and Philotheos, spent long periods of training on what was already then known as "the Holy Mountain." In the fourteenth century Mount Athos was

[31] Timothy Ware, *The Orthodox Church* (Penguin Books, 1993), p. 64.

[32] Ibid., p. 65, n. 2.

[33] Among the writings on the spiritual life popular at the time was one entitled *Peri ton tes Indias ethnon kai Brachmanon*. The Brahmins are described therein as devotees of uninterrupted prayer (*adialeiptos proseuche*): Grégoire Palamas, *Défense des saints hésychastes*, ed. J. Meyendorff, 2nd ed. (Louvain, 1973), I, xxxi, n. 6; J. Meyendorff, *Introduction à l'étude de Grégoire Palamas* (Paris, 1959), pp. 201–3; M. Eliade, *Yoga. Essai sur les origines de la mystique indienne* (Paris, 1936), pp. 86–8; idem, *Techniques du yoga* (Paris, 1948), p. 254.

a truly cosmopolitan centre, where Greeks, Slavs, Roumanians and other Orthodox peoples lived in close proximity to and, it would seem, reasonable amity with each other. Their common language was Greek; the *gerontes*, or teachers of the spiritual life, seem to have taught disciples of various nationalities. In the coenobitic houses of Athos, Slavs and Roumanians lived and worked alongside their Greek companions, studying, copying, and translating Greek religious (and sometimes secular) writings and relaying the new Slav versions to their native countries. Such Graeco-Slav communities also existed in this period in the monasteries of Constantinople (especially Stoudios) and Thessalonica, and in the two north Balkan monastic centres of Paroria and Kilifarevo which, no less than Mount Athos, became nurseries for the spread of Hesychasm in Eastern Europe.[34]

The region of Paroria, on the frontier between the Byzantine Empire and Bulgaria, became a noted "spiritual workshop" about 1330, when a great Byzantine ascetic, St. Gregory of Sinai, settled there with a group of monks whom he had instructed in "the prayer of the heart."[35] The group included Greeks, Bulgarians, and Serbs. Some were highly educated men who later rose to prominence in the churches of their respective lands. One of them was the Bulgarian monk Theodosius. After Gregory's death in 1346 he left Paroria, and eventually settled in Kilifarevo, on the northern slopes of the Balkan Mountains, not far from Trnovo, the Bulgarian capital. There, with the support of the Tsar John Alexander, he founded a

[34] See I. Dujcev, "Tsentry vizantiysko-slavyanskogo obshcheniya i sotrudnichestva", *Trudy Otdela Drevnerusskoy Literatury*, 19 (1963), pp. 107–29; idem, "Le Mont Athos et les Slaves au Moyen Age", in *Medioevo Bizantino-Slavo*, I (Rome, 1965), pp. 487–510.
[35] See Kallistos Ware, "The Jesus Prayer in St. Gregory of Sinai", *Eastern Churches Review*, 4 (1972), pp. 3–22.

monastic community modelled on the Paroria house. Kilifarevo soon inherited its predecessor's international role. Alongside native Bulgarians, Serbs, Hungarians, and Roumanians are mentioned there among Theodosius' disciples.

These Roumanian monks of Kilifarevo were probably responsible for spreading the teachings of Hesychasm north of the Danube. In the main, however, Roumanian Hesychasm came directly from Mount Athos, one of whose monasteries, Koutloumousiou, was placed under the patronage of a prince of Wallachia. The central figure in the transmission of Hesychasm to Wallachia in the second half of the fourteenth century was the monk Nikodemos. Born of a Greek father and a Serbian mother, he was trained as a monk on Mount Athos. Two famous Wallachian monasteries, Vodita and Tismana, owe their foundation to him.[36] With his Byzantine, Serbian, Roumanian, and Bulgarian connections, Nikodemos of Tismana is a living image of that cosmopolitan culture which, centred in Byzantium and cemented by Hesychasm, linked together the East European monasteries of the late Middle Ages. Before long Hesychasm penetrated still further north, to Moldavia. Neamtu, the country's leading medieval monastery, was founded in the late fourteenth century, probably by one of Nikodemos' disciples.

The Serbs, like the Bulgarians, seem to have owed their initiation into the doctrines and practice of Hesychasm largely to the Paroria school of Gregory of Sinai; though it is probable that their monasteries were touched by the mystical revival even earlier through the influence of the Serbian monastery of Hilandar on Mount Athos. Another monk of mixed Greek

---

[36] A.-E. Tachiaos, "Le mouvement hésychaste pendant les dernières décennies du XIVe siècle, *Kleronomia*, 6, 1 (1974), pp. 113–30.

and Slav descent, St. Romil of Vidin, a disciple of Gregory of Sinai in Paroria, moved to Mount Athos and thence (after 1375) to the Serbian monastery of Ravanica. He was a key figure in the transmission of Hesychasm to medieval Serbia.[37]

It is harder to gauge the impact of Byzantine Hesychasm on fourteenth century Russia. The evidence is analyzed with clarity and learning by John Meyendorff in his book *Byzantium and the Rise of Russia* (Cambridge, 1981).[38] Its teachings were probably accepted in Muscovy by the middle of the fourteenth century. Some of the evidence comes from the records of the Monastery of the Holy Trinity, founded in the middle of that century by St. Sergius of Radonezh, the most widely revered of Russian saints, some 70 kilometres north of Moscow, in what until recently was called Zagorsk and has now reverted to its original name Sergiev Posad. His disciple and biographer, the Russian monk Epiphanius, repeatedly refers to *bezmolvie* (literally "silence") and to the synonymous *molchanie*, practised by Sergius and his disciples. These Slavonic terms were used at that time as equivalents of the Greek *hesychia*. Corroborative evidence pointing to Sergius' involvement in the Hesychast movement is provided by his personal links with the Hesychast Patriarchs Philotheos and Kallistos; and by the presence in the library of the Trinity Monastery in the fourteenth and fifteenth centuries of Slavonic translations of many of the classics of Hesychast spirituality: among them were the works of

---

[37] See F. Halkin, "Un ermite des Balkans au XIVe siècle. *La Vie grecque inédite de Saint Romylos*", *Byzantion*, 31 (1961), pp. 111–47; P. Devos, "La version slave de la Vie de S. Romylos", ibid., 149–87. See also Tachiaos, "Le mouvement hésychaste", pp. 123–4, and E. Turdeanu, *La littérature bulgare du XIVe siècle et sa diffusion dans les pays roumains* (Paris, 1947), pp. 47–9.

[38] See also Tachiaos, *Epidraseis tou hesychasmou eis ten ekklesiastiken politikin en Rosia*, 1328–1406 (Thessaloniki, 1962).

John of the Ladder (Klimax), Isaac the Syrian, and Gregory of Sinai. In the second half of the fifteenth century Byzantine Hesychasm flowered again on Russian soil when St. Nil Sorsky, after visiting Mount Athos and Constantinople, revived the contemplative tradition in the forests to the north of the Volga. He seems to have been the first spiritual teacher in Russia to have taught his disciples to combine the practice of the "Jesus Prayer" with the psychosomatic methods used by the Balkan Hesychasts.[39] By the year 1400 a great centre of monastic settlement had arisen north of the upper Volga. The most famous of these houses was founded near Beloozero (the White Lake). In 1429 one of its monks settled on an island in the White Sea, laying the foundation of the monastery of Solovki: East Christian monasticism, still inspired by the Hesychast tradition, had reached the confines of the Arctic Ocean.

There is at first sight something surprising about the organisation of these late medieval Hesychast monasteries. The Hesychasts might have been expected to favour the eremitical, or at least the semi-eremitical, type of monasticism as more conducive to the practice of inner prayer. And indeed a number of *hesychasteria* did belong to this kind of settlement, typified by the *lavra* (in Greek), or the *skit* (in Slavonic). Gregory of Sinai and Gregory Palamas both lived this form of the monastic life on Mount Athos. Neither, however, believed that the practice of *hesychia* should be confined to those following the solitary life. There were advantages to be found in the coenobitic, or community, monasteries, whose members, living together in the same building, owning no personal property, were subject to the same discipline of prayer and work under the authority of an abbot—not least the virtue of spiritual obe-

---

[39] See F. von Lilienfeld, *Nil Sorskij und seine Schriften* (Berlin, 1963).

dience, by which the Hesychasts set great store. In fact Hesychasm greatly contributed to the revival of coenobitic monasticism in Eastern Europe.[40] Here is one example of this revival. About 1355 St. Sergius was visited by envoys from the Patriarch Philotheos, with a letter urging him to introduce the community rule into his monastery. Sergius, with the consent of the Russian primate Alexius, complied with this request. The Trinity Monastery, by adopting the Byzantine Studite constitution, became the model for many later *Koinobia* which arose in the forests of central and northern Russia. This network of coenobitic houses, whose monks often travelled long distances to visit some sister foundation, was a further factor in facilitating the spread of Hesychasm throughout Eastern Europe.

One of the meanings currently given to the term Hesychasm, you will recall, is the theology of St. Gregory Palamas. It would clearly be unprofitable to attempt in a few minutes an adequate summary of the thought and teachings of the chief exponent of Hesychast doctrines, even if I were capable of doing this. So I must confine myself to a few general points.[41] Firstly, it is important to realize that Palamas was no innovator. His teaching on mystical prayer can be traced back to fourth-century monastic practice on the one hand, and to patristic sources—notably Maximus the Confessor and Symeon the New Theologian—on the other. Secondly, Palamas laid great stress upon the vision of Divine Light. He defended the claim of the Hesychasts, past and present, to see this light with

[40] See G. M. Prokhorov, "Isikhazm i obshchestvennaya mysl' v vostochnoy Evrope v XIV veke", *Trudy Otdela Drevnerusskoy Literatury*, 23 (1968), pp. 86–108.

[41] On Hesychast theology see J. Meyendorff, *Introduction à l'étude de Grégoire Palamas* (Paris, 1959); idem, *A Study of Gregory Palamas* (London, 1964).

their bodily eyes, and held that it was identical with the Uncreated Light which the three disciples saw surrounding Jesus at his Transfiguration on Mount Tabor. Thirdly, to explain how God, transcendent and unknowable, can yet be perceived and approached by man, he distinguished between the essence and the energies of God. God's essence remains unknowable, but his uncreated energies—which are God himself—can be directly experienced by man in the form of grace. Palamas' teaching, after some controversy, was accepted as Orthodox at the church councils in Constantinople in 1341, 1347, and, with the strong support of the reigning Emperor John VI Cantacuzenos, in 1351.

What Meyendorff has called this "original synthesis of the patristic tradition" was not unknown outside Byzantium. Yet it may seem surprising, in view of the readiness of the Slavs to adopt the tenets of Hesychasm, that the theology of Gregory Palamas seems to have had little impact on Slav countries in the late Middle Ages. It was from Gregory of Sinai, not from Gregory Palamas, that most medieval Slav readers derived their knowledge of Byzantine Hesychasm. The Serbs seem to have been an exception: it was in fourteenth century Serbia that Palamas' writings were first translated into Slavonic; and the Serbs began to venerate him as a saint even before his official canonisation in 1368.[42]

If the spiritual impulse which caused the expansion of the Hesychast movement came from Athos and other Balkan monasteries, the movement was given an administrative structure and organisational support by the Patriarchate of Constantinople. Out of the seven patriarchs who occupied the oecumenical throne between 1351 and the end of the century,

---

[42] See J. Meyendorff, *Introduction*, pp. 334–5; Tachiaos, "Le mouvement hésychaste", p. 126.

six belonged to the Hesychast movement. Most of them were far from unworldly. They shunned neither social nor political activity; they fought, often vigorously, against state interference in ecclesiastical appointments; and they displayed a remarkable zest for church administration. Much of their effort was directed to maintaining and strengthening the authority of the Byzantine Patriarchate over the Slav churches of Eastern Europe. In the fourteenth century the Patriarch's authority, in documents issued by his chancellery, was often defined as *kedemonia panton* (that is "guardianship" of, or "solicitude" for, all). The Patriarch of Constantinople, in a document of the time, is called "the common father and teacher of the entire world (*koinos pasis tis oikoumenes patir kai didaskalos*). This doctrine was given forceful expression in a letter, written in 1370, by the Patriarch Philotheos to the princes of Russia. "God," wrote the Patriarch, "has appointed our humility (*ten hemon metriotita*) as the leader of the Christians of the whole world and the guardian and curator of their souls; all are dependent on me, the father and teacher of all. … Since, however, it is not possible for one man … to go the round of the world, our humility chooses the best men and those most distinguished in virtue, and appoints and consecrates them pastors and teachers and bishops, and sends them to the various parts of the world."[43] This, and similar patriarchal declarations, which would not have come amiss from the pen of an enthusiastic champion of papal supremacy in the Roman Curia, aimed to instill in their Slav recipients the conviction that Orthodox Christendom was a single body whose head was the Oecumenical Patriarch.

[43] *Acta Patriarchatus Constantinopolitani*, ed. F. Miklosisich and I. Muller, I (Vienna, 1860) pp. 520–22; Meyendorff, *Byzantium and the Rise of Russia* (Cambridge, 1981), pp. 283–4.

It was these prelates, above all, who inherited from the now largely impotent Byzantine government the role of chief spokesman of its imperial traditions. Their chosen instruments in this imperial and pan-Orthodox policy were Hesychast monks, many of them Slavs, who—by training and conviction—could be relied upon to uphold the authority of the oecumenical patriarchate among their flocks, and to resist the growth of local forms of nationalism. It is not surprising to find that the leaders of the pro-Byzantine, pan-Orthodox parties in the different Slav countries all belonged to the Hesychast movement. In Bulgaria they proved strong enough to withstand the forces of nationalism and, despite a major crisis which erupted between Constantinople and Trnovo between 1355 and 1375, were able to prevent a permanent rift in the structure of the Byzantine Commonwealth.[44] An even more serious schism between the Byzantine and Serbian Churches was caused by the coronation in 1346 of the Serbian monarch Stephen Dusan as "Emperor and Autocrat of Serbia and Roumania". It was healed in 1375 by the action of a group of Serbian Hesychasts. Their leader, the Serbian monk Isaiah, equally renowned among Greeks and Slavs, enjoyed the friendship of the Patriarch Philotheos.[45]

Philotheos was certainly the most influential and successful of Hesychast leaders. He was fortunate enough to secure, as his agent in Lithuania and Muscovy, the support of the Bulgarian monk Cyprian, one of the most striking personalities of the second half of the fourteenth century.[46] Successively an

[44] *Acta Patriarchatus Constantinopolitani*, I, pp. 436–42; P. A. Syrku, *K istorii ispravleniya knig v Bolgarii v XIV veke*, I, (St. Petersburg, 1898), p. 57.

[45] See Tachiaos, "Le mouvement hésychaste", pp. 122–5.

[46] See D. Obolensky, *Six Byzantine Portraits* (Oxford, 1988), pp. 173–200; Meyendorff, *Byzantium and the Rise of Russia*, pp. 200–25.

Athonite monk, a representative of Philotheos as metropolitan in Kiev, a victim of the political rivalry between Muscovy and Lithuania, and, in the end, from 1390 to 1406, the incumbent of the see of Moscow, Cyprian epitomizes in the breadth of his mental horizon and in his multiple loyalties the rich cosmopolitan culture which flourished in Eastern Europe during the late Middle Ages. He skillfully pursued, often to his own detriment, the policy of his patron, the Patriarch Philotheos. As a Byzantine agent in Russia he proved useful as a fund-raiser; he inserted into Russian liturgical practice the new articles of the Byzantine *Synodicon* which endorsed the theology of the Hesychasts, thus contributing to the spread of their doctrines in Russia; and he played a crucial role in the famous conflict which broke out in the 1390s between the grand prince of Moscow, Basil I, and the oecumenical patriarch Antony IV. In 1393 the patriarch wrote a letter to the Muscovite ruler, rebuking him for banning the commemoration of the emperor's name from the liturgy of the Russian Church. He took a particularly grave view of the statement by the Russian ruler: "We have the Church, but not the emperor." Mindful of his duty as (in his words) "the universal teacher of all Christians", the patriarch reiterated the basic principle of Byzantine political philosophy: "The holy emperor," he writes, "is not as other rulers and governors of other regions are. ... He is anointed with the great chrism, and is elected *basileus* and *avtokrator* of the Romans, that is, of all Christians."[47]

Historians have often pointed out that the Patriarch Antony's letter is a classic exposition of the Byzantine doctrine of the universal East Roman Empire, ruled by the *basileus ton*

---

[47] *Acta Patriarchatus Constantinopolitani*, II, pp. 188–92; English transl. E. Barker, *Social and Political Thought in Byzantium* (Oxford, 1957), pp. 194–6, who mistakenly renders "*myron*" as "myrrh".

Romaion, earthly vicegerent of God, supreme lawgiver in Christendom, whose authority was held to extend over all Christian rulers and peoples. Usually indeed, Antony's words have been taken at their face value, and Basil I's refusal to allow the emperor's name to be inscribed in the commemorative diptychs of the Russian Church has been regarded as a nationalistic revolt against Byzantine claims to universal hegemony, and thus a revolutionary break with tradition. In recent years, however, John Meyendorff has argued that it was Cyprian, not Basil I, who was innovating; and that, in the teeth of conservative opposition led by the Russian ruler, he was trying to introduce into Moscovy the novel practice of commemorating the emperor's name in the churches of the land. No sure conclusion on this matter seems possible until the Slavonic liturgical books used in Russia during the Middle Ages are published and studied; and in default of new evidence, the question remains an open one. We can, however, be certain of two things: in this conflict between Moscow and Constantinople, Cyprian took the Byzantine side; secondly, he won in the end, for he wrote about 1397 that the emperor is commemorated liturgically in the churches of Moscow.[48]

I spoke earlier of the influence exerted by Hesychasm on the literature of Eastern Europe in the late Middle Ages. A few words are needed to confirm this point. In the second half of the fourteenth century a notable increase in literary production can be observed in several East European countries. It owed much of its original impulse to Euthymius, Patriarch of Trnovo. A Bulgarian by birth, he joined the monastic community of Kilifarevo, where he became the leading disciple of St. Theodosius. Active as a writer, he revised the Slavonic versions of the church service books, translated several liturgical

[48] Meyendorff, *Byzantium and the Rise of Russia*, pp. 254–6.

texts from Greek into Slavonic, and wrote biographies and panegyrics of several Byzantine and Bulgarian saints. The literary school founded by Euthymius seems to have aimed at the wholesale replacement of the earlier Slavonic versions of the sacred texts—including the Scriptures—by a new corpus of translations from the Greek. The new translations were expected to conform more closely to the grammar, spelling and punctuation of the early translations by Cyril and Methodius, and also to the morphology and syntax of their Greek originals. Euthymius' independent writings set the guidelines of what became the standard literary style of Slavic hagiography and panegyrics of the late Middle Ages: a style emphatic, rhetorical, and ornate, striving for emotional and acoustic effect by frequent resort to exclamations and repetitions. These "literary" reforms became the common patrimony of the Bulgarians, the Serbs, the Roumanians and the Russians.[49]

This readiness of churchmen to tamper with the very texts of Holy Writ may seem surprising. Yet in several respects—notably in its idealization of the Church Slavonic past and its appeal to the authority of Byzantine models—this programme of linguistic reform was rooted in the outlook of East European intellectuals of the time. In the troubled world of late fourteenth century Balkan politics, the growing power of the Ottoman Turks could be seen as a consequence of the spiritual disunity and moral decline of Christians. A sense of impending doom and a despondent belief that the present times were inferior to the glorious past were then fairly widespread in Byzantium. The idea that the corruption of morals was a result of a corruption in the spelling of manuscripts may seem far-

---

[49] *Werke des Patriarchen von Bulgarien Euthymius (1375–1393)*, ed. E. Kaluzniacki(Vienna, 1901) (Variorum Reprints, 1971); E. Turdeanu, *La littérature bulgare du XIVe siècle*, pp. 67–135; *Trnovska Knizhovna Shkola*, ed. P. Rusev and others (Sofia, 1974).

fetched to the modern mind; yet, at a time of widespread belief in the literal truth of the sacred texts of Christianity and in the supernatural efficacy of ritual, the knowledge that the accuracy of the former and the purity of the latter were in jeopardy could easily generate a feeling of acute anxiety. In this situation of near panic, it was perhaps only natural to conclude that the salvation of the individual and of society lay in the "correction" of books and ritual, in the promotion of the unity of Orthodox Christendom, and in the striving for spiritual perfection. These conclusions were in fact widely drawn in Hesychast circles between 1350 and 1450.

The debt which this literary movement owes to Byzantine Hesychasm has been explored by a distinguished Russian scholar, Prof. D. S. Likhachev.[50] Three of his arguments seem to me persuasive: firstly, most of the religious texts translated from Greek into Church Slavonic in the fourteen and fifteenth centuries, and which came to fill the monastic libraries of Eastern Europe, were ascetic and spiritual writings popular in Hesychast circles: they included works by John of the Ladder, Isaac the Syrian, Symeon the New Theologian, Gregory of Sinai and the Patriarch Kallistos. Some of these works, translated for the first time, brought their Slav readers into contact with the *avant-garde* literature of Byzantium; others, already familiar in earlier translations, were retranslated in the period: among them was "The Ladder" (*Klimax*), whose new Slavic version was produced in Serbia, probably c.1370, and played a major role in the spread of Hesychast spirituality throughout Eastern Europe.[51]

---

[50] D. S. Likhachev, *Razvitie russkoy literatury X–XVII vekov* (Leningrad, 1973), pp. 93–102.
[51] See D. Bogdanovic:, *Jovan Lestvicnik u vizantijskoj i staroj srpskoj knijizevnosti* (Belgrade, 1968), especially pp. 28–9, 172, 194–6, 200.

Secondly, Hesychast doctrines and practices were widely disseminated in Eastern Europe by hagiographical writings. Some of the leading Byzantine Hesychasts, notably the Patriarchs Kallistos and Philotheos, were enthusiastic writers of saints' lives, and used them to propagate the ideal of *hesychia*. Their Slav collaborators followed suit. Better than abstruse theological treatises, the biographies of saints who had devoted their lives to "the prayer of the heart" could publicize among the Slavs the values of the Hesychast tradition. It is not surprising that hagiography became the most popular literary genre of the period. Some of these saint's biographies seem to have stemmed from a bilingual Graeco-Slav environment. Thus the *Vita* of St. Romil of Vidin, composed in the late fourteenth century, has come down to us in a Greek and in a Slavonic version, and it is quite possible that it was written simultaneously in both languages.[52]

Thirdly, the urge to "correct" the liturgical books by removing the scribes' errors and bringing the texts into line with the Greek originals, also had roots in the Hesychast movement. The Hesychasts showed a lively interest in matters of ritual and their "purist" attitude led them to work for a purification and a renewal of the Church's liturgical life. This concern for liturgical reform, to cite one instance, was imparted to the Russians by their Hesychast metropolitan Cyprian.

The role played by this late medieval literary movement— a movement at once antiquarian, elitist, philhellenic, and cosmopolitan—was summarized by D. S. Likhachev in these

---

[52] See I. Dujcev, "Rapports littéraires entre les Byzantins, les Bulgares et les Serbes aux XIVe et XVe siècles," in *L'Ecole de la Morava et son temps* (Belgrade, 1972), p. 90; idem, "Slawische Heilige in der byzantinischen Hagiographie", *Südost-Forschungen*, 19 (1960), pp. 83–4.

words: "We are confronted with the phenomenon of a single intellectual movement, sufficiently powerful to embrace various countries and sufficiently profound to have affected simultaneously literature, writing, painting and religion."[53]

The possible relationship, hinted at here, between Hesychasm and Palaeologan painting of the fourteenth and fifteenth centuries raises complex problems which have been much debated of late. I have neither the time nor the technical expertise to discuss this problem here. I will confine myself to two general remarks. Firstly, the attempts of several modern scholars to demonstrate the influence of Hesychasm on Palaeologan art, though frequently ingenuous, seem to me inconclusive. Secondly, it can scarcely be doubted that Palaeologan art, an art primarily religious in content, could not have escaped the influence of the contemporary and equally cosmopolitan Hesychast movement which had so profound an impact on East European culture in the late Middle Ages.[54]

In the last resort, however, I should probably repeat the note of warning I sounded at the outset of this paper. In an important article published in 1983 and entitled "Is Hesychasm the Right Word?" the late John Meyendorff cautioned against using the term too loosely.[55] But, provided we avoid the popular and misleading associations of Hesychasm with what he calls "anachoretism, obscurantism, or esoteric mysticism," he does allow its use in a broader sense. "It has become," he writes, "a convenient and probably irreplaceable term encompassing a broad religious and political movement which struggled for a

---

[53] D. S. Likhachev, "Nekotorye zadachi izucheniya vtorogo yuzhnoslavyanskogo vliyaniya v Rossii", in *Issledovaniya po slavyanskomu literaturovedeniu i folkloristike* (Moscow, 1960), p. 107.
[54] See Obolensky, *The Byzantine Commonwealth* (1971), pp. 358–9.
[55] *Harvard Ukrainian Studies*, 7 (1983), pp. 447–56.

common set of values, promoted political and cultural priorities inherited from Byzantium, and, in the face of challenges coming from the East and the West, maintained the universalism and the dynamism of Orthodox Christianity amidst drastic social and political changes."

The monasteries of Eastern Europe, the pan-Orthodox policy of the Hesychast Patriarchs of Constantinople, and the literary movement of the late Middle Ages were the sinews by which the cultural cohesion of the Byzantine Commonwealth was maintained during the final century of its history. In the last resort, however, the decisive role in maintaining this unity—and in ensuring the continuing dialogue between Byzantium and the Slavs—was played by individuals. Some of them have already been mentioned. In these brief concluding remarks I hope to show that the efficacy as intermediaries of these men was much enhanced by two characteristics which they shared: the personal bonds of friendship or discipleship which linked them together within a single international community; and their astonishing mobility.

The willingness of these Hesychast monks to travel widely would have astonished their Benedictine contemporaries, bound by the rule of stability, though not their distant Irish predecessors. Many Hesychasts were great travellers. The motives which prompted their travels were varied: among them were an urge to seek qualified teachers of *hesychia*, the desire to spread the knowledge of "the prayer of the heart," and sometimes the more mundane wish to escape the embarrassing consequences of worldly fame. This movement was given a further impetus in the late fourteenth century by the Ottoman advance in the Balkans. After the battle of Kosovo (1389) and the fall of Trnovo (1393) the northward movement of refugees, seeking to escape the Turkish invasion, gathered momentum. To judge their role in proper perspective, we should recognize that these monks, churchmen, and scholars moved within the same cultural area, whose unity had recently been strengthened by the spread of Hesychasm and of Euthymius' literary reforms. In migrating from one part of the Byzantine Commonwealth to another they expected to find, and generally did, similar conditions for their scholarly work and ecclesiastical activity.

Their effectiveness as acculturators was enhanced by the strength and endurance of their personal links. During the hundred years between 1325 and 1425 four generations of prominent Hesychasts succeeded each other on the East European scene: Gregory of Sinai was the spiritual master of Theodosius of Trnovo; the latter was the teacher of the Patriarch Euthymius who, in his turn, was the mentor of Gregory Tsamblak, another Hesychast grandee. If it is remembered that, in Eastern Christian monasticism, the relationship between teacher and disciple is the most sacred and unbreakable of human bonds, this spiritual genealogy will be seen as evidence of an impressive continuity of precept and practice. Each of these men, in addition, had personal links with fellow Hesychasts, at home and abroad: the Patriarch Kallistos was a disciple of Gregory of Sinai, and a friend of both Theodosius and Euthymius; the Patriarch Philotheos was Cyprian's mentor; Cyprian was (in all probability) a pupil of Thedosius and (certainly) a friend of Euthymius; while Euthymius, apart from his contacts with colleagues in Bulgaria, on Mount Athos and in Constantinople, was in correspondence with Nikodemos of Tismana in Wallachia. These leading figures in the Hesychast movement, though often dispersed throughout Eastern Europe, remained in close touch with each other. Many shared a common loyalty to a spiritual *alma mater*, such as Mount Athos, Paroria or

Sir Dimitri Obolensky

Kilifarevo. Most of them were linked, in successive generations, with one or the other of the great names of the Hesychast movement: with Gregory of Sinai, Theodosius of Trnovo, the Patriarchs Kallistos, Philotheos, and Euthymius, with Sergius of Moscow and with Cyprian—men who (together with Gregory Palamas) dominated this movement with the same authority which Cyril and Methodius and their immediate disciples had enjoyed among the Slavs of the early Middle Ages. And, belonging as they did to the supra-national community which the Roumanian scholar Alexander Elian has called "the Hesychast International",[56] they all, directly or by proxy, retained contact with the religious and cultural life of Byzantium, whose hagiographical literature and Hesychast spirituality remained models

[56] "Byzance et les Roumains", *Proceedings of the Thirteenth International Congress of Byzantine Studies* (Oxford, 1966) (London, 1967), p. 199.

Preservation Through Translation: Reflections on Tradition and Traditions

The Very Reverend Leonidas C. Contos

Some years ago Vladimir Lossky, the eminent Orthodox theologian, co-authored, with Leonid Ouspensky, *The Meaning of Icons.* He entitled his preface "Tradition and Traditions," and he begins by saying: "Tradition is one of those terms which, through being too rich in meanings, runs the risk of finally having none." He concedes that this may be due in part to a certain "secularization" which has depreciated so much of the theological vocabulary, words like *"spirituality," "mystical," "communion,"* "detaching them from their Christian context in order to make of them the current coin of profane language." He suggests that if we try to avoid mutilating the idea by keeping all its various meanings intact, we are reduced to definitions which embrace too many things at once but fail to convey the real meaning of tradition.

The first and essential note of any definition of tradition is that it is living, that so long as the Church exists, this living tradition will remain a cardinal mark, being the perpetual need to understand and interpret, and live out, the meaning of Christian truth in the changing context of the Church's life.

The evidence is ample that the Apostles themselves understood the importance of this; they are constantly reminding the faithful of it. Writes St. Paul to the Thessalonians: "So then, brethren, stand firm and hold to the traditions . . ." (1

Thess. 2:15). Elsewhere to the Church at Corinth: "I commend you because you remember me in everything and maintain the traditions even as I delivered them to you." (1 Cor. 11:2). Then to Timothy: ". . . and what have you heard from me before many witnesses, entrust to faithful men who will be able to teach others also." (2 Tim. 1:13, 2:2).

There is hardly a word here that can be overlooked, whose meaning is not vital to the idea of tradition: *stand firm, hold, remember, maintain, delivered, heard, witnesses, entrust, teach others.*

A key word is *witness.* Papias, a first century Bishop, whom Irenaeus identified as *archaios aner*, a man of long ago, reflects this attitude of the early Church: "If ever anyone came who had followed the presbyters, I inquired of them what Peter or Andrew or Philip or Thomas or James or John or Matthew, or any of the Lord's disciples had said."

Now all this may sound like an argument for antiquity as an essential synonym for tradition. That would be true only in part. It is not what the adjective "living" means. It is to St. Basil the great that we owe the most nearly perfect definition. In his *Treatise on the Holy Spirit* there is this well-known passage: "Among the doctrines and teachings preserved by the Church, we hold some from written sources, and we have collected others transmitted in an unexplicit form from apostolic tradition." The Greek for "unexplicit" is the adverb *mystikos,* which can mean secretly, i.e., hidden, or as it often does, sacramentally.

What is implied here is that while Scripture was known to all, yet within the Church there was an inner tradition familiar only to the initiate, related to the inner, the sacramental, life of the closed Christian community. St. Basil insists on their interdependence, their essential unity, their equal force: "They have all the same value . . . For if we were to try to put aside the unwritten customs as having no great force, we should, unknown to ourselves, be weakening the Gospel in its very essence; we should, moreover, be transforming the *kerygma* into mere word."

One even slightly acquainted with the Orthodox liturgical mode will note its open and solemn veneration of the Bible as central to all worship. It consists in much more than reading biblical lections. The many various services, the Divine Liturgy included, are densely woven with elements of the Psalms and the prophecies. To comprehend Orthodox hymnology demands a true intimacy with the Old Testament. To be sure, veneration is directed more to Gospel, more specifically the Book of the Gospels, which occupies a place of honor on the Holy Altar, close to the reserved Sacrament, is censed and kissed and carried high in procession as the ultimate icon of the Lord made manifest in His Word.

But veneration of this "icon," unlike that paid to images of holy people, or holy events, is of a unique duality: it is profound respect for the object, *proskynesis*, but worship, *latreia*, of its content. For that content is the revealed Truth. Totally alien to Orthodox thought is the notion that the Bible may be regarded as a theological encyclopedia, to be found definitely stated. Hence Basil's statement: "We do not content ourselves with what was reported in the *Apostolos*, (the Lectionary of the Epistles and the Acts), and in the Gospels; but both before and after reading them we add other doctrines (read *teachings*), received from oral teaching and carrying much weight in the mystery [of the faith]."

What does he mean by these "other doctrines?" We are to understand these as the liturgical, the sacramental traditions. Such essential data are not provided directly, or fully, by the inspired writers, in part at least because they considered them self-evident. But if we were to ignore the fact that first-century Christians practiced Baptism and performed the Eucharist, we would be at a loss to understand, or at best would not fully comprehend, Jesus' sayings on the Bread of Heaven, the Vine, of water springing up eternal life – granted the sacramental interpretation of such passages is not the only one possible.

Clearly then, though complete in itself, Scripture presupposes Tradition, not as something added to it, but as the very context within which it becomes fully intelligible and "effective for salvation." Therefore, to be fully understood, authentically interpreted, the Bible requires the reality of that communion which is the Church. Thus Tradition has been defined as "the sacramental continuity, in history, of the communion of saints, in this sense of the Church itself."

Continuity, then, may be the operative word. It can have many synonyms. Collective memory may be one. Self-identity another. Self-preservation yet another. The Church was always mindful not to confuse the one Sacred Tradition, which not only constitutes but safeguards her self-identity through the ages, with what the Lord Himself condemned as accretions in the Historical Church, sometimes creative and positive, sometimes not. Even in the intense heat of Greek-Latin disputes over rites and practices, there were those who never lost sight of the vital distinctions between the capital "T" and the small, between the singular and the plural.

Photios, Patriarch in the late 9th century, was condemned by Pope Nicholas I on the basis of canonical norms unknown in the East. He wisely proclaimed the principle that all legitimate local traditions might coexist in the Universal Church. "Everybody must preserve what was defined by common ecumenical decisions," he writes to the Pope, "but a particular opinion of a Church Father, or a definition issued by a local council, can be followed by some and ignored by others." To illustrate the absurd depths to which the debate had fallen, he makes specific mention of shaving and not shaving, fasting on Saturdays, married clergy, etc. "When the faith remains inviolate, the common and catholic decisions are also safe; a sensible man respects the practices and laws of other; he considers that it is neither wrong to observe them, nor illegal to violate them."

But there can be a dark side to this. Just as the debates between Rome and Constantinople in the 9th century turned on norms unknown to the East, so from the 17th century, a period that was critical for Orthodox theology, the East deviated from the patristic norm and underwent influences from the West. It was a conscious, indeed a self-conscious and in a sense unnatural, attempt at self-explanation after a long isolation. So there was borrowing, rather eclectic, of habits and schemes of thought from late Roman Scholasticism, as well as from various currents of the Reformation. It all had desultory consequences for Orthodox theology.

Of this phenomenon Father Georges Florovsky has this to say: "The *style of theology has changed.* Yet this did not imply any change in doctrine. It is indeed a sore and ambiguous *pseudomorphosis* of Eastern theology, which is not yet overcome even in our time. This *pseudomorphosis* meant a certain splint in the soul of the East, to borrow one of Arnold Toynbee's favorite expressions." Father Florovsky states the obvious, of course, yet it needs to be restated: that in the life of the Church such a split, such a loss of self-identity, is, in the end, fatal for Orthodoxy. In spite of occasional deviations, in spite of the accidents of history, the Tradition has never been lost; the whole structure of Eastern Liturgy – in the inclusive sense of the word – is still thoroughly patristic. It is in this exact sense that it must be said that the so-called "age of the Fathers" is not an age at all; it is the spirit that animates the worshipping Church, which is to say the living Church. Florovsky then asks:

> Should it not continue also in the schools, in the field of theological research and instruction? Should we not recover the "mind of the Fathers" also in our theological thinking and confession? Recover, indeed, not as an archaic pose and habit, and not just as a venerable relic, but as a existential attitude, as a spiritual orientation. Actually, we are living already in an age of revival and restoration. Yet it is not enough to keep a 'Byzantine' Liturgy, to restore a 'Byzantine style' in iconography and church architecture, to practice 'Byzantine' modes of prayer and self-discipline. One has to go back to the very roots of this traditional 'piety,' which has always been cherished as a holy inheritance.

Inheritance inescapably calls forth all those words whose meanings, we agreed, are vital to the idea of tradition – *hold, maintain, remember* – and above all – *deliver, entrust, teach*. And surely not forgetting father Florovsky's *cherish*, which means to value, hold dear, cling to. An inheritance is not merely something that may or may not be passed on as a legal right from one's predecessors, to be used or abused at the will or the whim of the successor. Rather, it inheres to, is inherent in, the identity of that family, or community, which possesses it.

You will remember from the Parable of the Prodigal that he squandered his "property," in the King James Version his "substance," which is more faithful to the Greek *ousia*. Later in the narrative the embittered older son refers to it as tovn bivon, your very life. Once we have ceased to think of our tradition, our inheritance, as our very life, that which inheres to our very being, which informs our very identity, then all talk of preservation becomes superfluous.

I have adopted as a title for this talk "Preservation Through

Translation." If you will indulge me one more slight but very necessary etymological excursus, "to translate" has, for our purposes, more than the obvious and familiar meaning: to express the sense of a word or a book or a poem in another language. It has, for example, an ecclesiastical meaning, as when a bishop is translated to another see, or the relics of a saint are moved from one place to another, in which latter case we speak of it as "recovery," a "restoration" — *anakomiden*, a "bringing back" of that which has been lost.

Perhaps more to the point of this discussion is one further meaning of translate, oddly enough a mechanical one: "causing a body to move so that all its parts travel in the same direction." Given a tendency for going off in all directions, that may not be as odd a definition as it sounds.

And now we need to define what exactly it is that we must carefully and faithfully translate so that, whatever changes of place, or climate or circumstance may occur, it continues to be intelligible, it remains part of our collective, unbroken memory, an unmistakable mark of who we are, what we have been, what we see it as our destiny to remain.

Inevitably this brings us back to where we began, defining Tradition as "*the sacramental continuity, in history, of the communion of saints – of the Church itself.*" Going back, as Florovsky rightly has it, to the very roots that "traditional piety" which has always been cherished as a holy inheritance.

If we agreed that this is a "sacramental continuity," I would suggest that it can be embraced in three main categories: first, where we worship; second, what is unique to that worship; and third, the idiom of that worship. Or, to put it otherwise: architecture, iconography, hymnology. Each in its function, and all together, to the degree that they are faithfully preserved – *translated* – are the authentic expression of the Orthodox faith.

Orthodox Church Architecture

From earliest times, once the Church emerged from the underground, Christian communities began to build churches, most commonly over the tombs of their Martyrs, or places to which the Martyrs' relics were "translated." At first they borrowed and adapted, mainly from the public buildings of late Roman times. But by the 6th century, even before Justinian's Great Church of the Divine Wisdom, the concept of the Christian empire as the earthly reflection of the celestial kingdom (imperfect to be sure) began to be articulated in the churches of the Christian East, and in their interior art.

They are not only distinctive, never to be mistaken for other than what they are; notwithstanding a marvelous variety in mass and form, they possess an inherent harmony that owes less to physical shape than to sacred purpose. Whether you study the Church of Saints Sergius and Bacchus, or Saint Euphemia, or the magnificent *Aghia Irene*, hard by *Aghia Sophia* (where the Turks recently staged a beauty contest); whether you consider the powerful churches of Ravenna or the miniature jewels to be to be discovered in the valleys and mountain fastnesses of Greece and Serbia, or in their hundreds on the sun-drenched islands of the Aegean; or even if you stumble across an *ermoklesi*, lovingly if clumsily built of adobe by a single pair of untrained hands, and regularly whitewashed – each is an attempt, conscious or intuitive, to preserve, to translate, that "sacramental continuity, in history, of the communion of saints, in this sense of the Church itself."

In recent times we have been in the midst of a ferment of building with millions of our *ousia* spent on churches and community buildings. I have been happily spared the visual affront of seeing all of them, but I have seen enough inverted bowls and cartoon stained glass windows (stained glass windows!)

and colonnades that relate to nothing, go nowhere, and peristyles that support nothing, and flying domes of every shape, some like nuclear reactors, formless forms that neither follow nor serve a function – all in the name of a confused style blithely called "Neo-Byzantine," whatever that is supposed to mean; enough to support the sad conclusion that we are not only very far from the "roots of our traditional piety," but seem determined to uproot all vestiges of our holy inheritance.

ORTHODOX ICONOGRAPHY

The situation with iconography is rather less calamitous. Not that there have not been aberrations. One thinks of the Russian school of a certain period, or of the mass production of the Ioasaphaioi, with their Christ like Pre-Raphaelite Galahads, tawny locks gently waved, looking nothing so much as Clairol ads; of Archangels, far from heralds of God's Word to man, but simpering seraphs that seem to have stepped out of Victorian valentines. Whether there has been a subtle process of education, or more and better iconographers are now at work, our instinct for the icon has undergone a redemptive corrective.

It may just be that Western eyes have in recent decades discovered the icon, albeit more as a decorative element than just as an object of piety. Whatever the case, its mystical, otherworldly power as a "place of the gracious presence" has imposed itself anew on our consciousness. For here after all is where we encounter the divine, where God's holy men and women hold discourse with us.

ORTHODOX HYMNOLOGY

The two terms are purposely juxtaposed. They are forces that interpenetrate each other, that co-inhere to that sacramental continuity of which we are speaking; together they are our theological language. It is often said that our theology is essentially hymnological, our hymnology is essentially theological. The visitor will find no such thing as an Orthodox hymnal, all the hymns for all occasions and seasons neatly alphabetized. What the inquirer may find, eventually and after an arduous guided search, is a vast body of devotional poetry – some of it mediocre and a bit forced, I grant you, but much of it of a very high order, even exalted – the product of many centuries, the inspiration of celebrated melodists and anonymous monastics alike, of Patriarchs, even the occasional Emperor.

I have suggested that our "Holy inheritance" may be seen in the three main categories of where we worship, of what is unique to that worship, and finally, of the language in which we worship. This third is the most difficult proposition of all. Fads and fashions in architecture and icon painting are, in the end, transient. The eye soon tells us what rings false. The innovative eventually is embarrassed by the integrity of the authentic. But language, the instrument on which we accompany our hearts and minds in worship, this is another matter.

It has been suggested that liturgical language, that is, the sacramental word, is nothing less than verbal iconography. A verbal icon, not unlike a graphic one, deserves to be approached with much the same awe and humility that the painter brings to this task, accompanied by prayer and fasting and, above all, the consciousness that he is not creating an original work, but only preserving, restoring, making freshly intelligible, the received and the cherished. His medium must be pure, his pigments the brightest and most luminous, yet his palette seemly and sober.

The issue of liturgical translations is most posited as between *old* and *new*. That is not the question. The issue is between language that is adequate for understanding as against language that is adequate to the Mystery. It is not enough that it be accurate, though certainly it must faithfully convey the original; it must have the grace and cadence of poetry, be able to satisfy the intellect, but also speak to the heart.

There is a persistent and wrong-headed notion that the Greek into which the Hebrew Scriptures were translated about the second century B.C. was just the common street language of the time. *Koine* does indeed mean common, but in the sense of universal, thus closely related to *koinonia*, communion.

True, it was the Common Greek of the ancient world, the language of commerce and business; that does not mean it was the idiom of the docks or the wine shops. It was filtered and refined, a language of immense subtlety and power, an exquisite language at its very best.

It is like saying that the language of the King James Bible or the Coverdale Psalter is merely street English of the late 16th and early 17th centuries, or that Shakespeare wrote his plays and those transcendent sonnets in the bawdy tongue of Elizabethan public houses. Nothing could be farther from the truth. It is vigorous Tudor English elevated into artistic works that never cease to astonish us.

Equally astonishing, for the richness of their imagery and the power of their rhythm, are many of our hymns. Given the complexities of syntax, pressed to fit fixed melodic models, and the unfamiliarity of their vocabulary, they are not accessible to the average worshiper. But unveiling their meanings, making their poets our contemporaries, is like mining for gold. Let me offer four random examples.

The *Troparion of Kassiane*, sung Tuesday evening of Holy Week, Orthros for Wednesday, was in fact composed as a poem by a 9th century nun, a gifted hymnographer. Its theme is the repentant harlot who in Matthew's account poured priceless ointment over the head of Jesus as He was supping in the house of Simon the Leper, bathed His feet with her tears, then dried them with her hair.

"Lord, the woman caught up in multitude of sins, sensing Your divinity, assumes the perfumer's role; lamenting, she provides myrrh in anticipation of Your burial." But then we hear the anguished voice of the woman herself: "Alas!," she cries, "for me night is a frenzy of excess, dark and moonless, a love affair with sin."

Suddenly the images take on a broader sweep: "You draw from the clouds the water of the sea; will you accept the fountainhead of my tears. In your inexpressible condescension You made the very heavens incline; incline now to the groaning of my heart."

Once again the figures become close and personal, the focus immediate: "I will cover Your spotless feet with kisses, then dry them with my tresses."

Just as abruptly as before the image turns cosmic. This is no longer a lone woman taken in sin. The word "feet" calls up a whole new image. She is all woman, all humankind, all Eve herself, and the scene is the lost Eden. A one-syllable pronoun signals the shift: *on, en to* . . . . – Here the syntax can hardly be rendered; the best we can do is this: As God paced Paradise in the twilight, His footfalls echoed like thunderclaps in Eve's ears, sending her hiding in terror. And now the soliloquy of a wretched woman turns again within herself, and on the infinite distance between her fallenness and the divine compassion: "Who can fathom, who can measure, the multitude of my sins against the depths of Your judgments?" The majestic poem ends with the petition that He who has boundless mercy will not reject His handmaid in her abject and moving confession.

As the first example illustrates the power of penitential tears, this second conveys the Church's tenderness in the face of tears of bereavement. Two verses from the Funeral Service for Infants, sung as the faithful offer their last respects:

"Who would not lament, my child, your sad departure from this life? For yet an infant before your time flew swift as a swallow to find a refuge with the creator of all. O child, who could ever fail to grieve, seeing your tender face, like a delicate rose so soon faded?

"Who would not bemoan, child, you perfect comeliness, not bewail the beauty of your pure life? Like some fleet ship that leaves no wake, so swiftly have you slipped from my sight."

The third illustration is but one example of the Church's devotion to the Theotokos, a theme of which she never tires. It is the *Doxastikon* of the Fifth Tone. It is important to note that these are also called *Dogmatika*, each one being a concise little theological treatise. This one has special poetic quality and, like so much of our hymnology, draws on Old Testament typology, in this case on the crossing of the Red Sea.

"Upon the Red Sea an image of the Virgin Bride was once drawn." The poet then altered images, from the Old Dispensation to the New, and as he does so we are struck by how skillfully he employs all the poetic devices – alliteration, juxtaposition, rhyme. "There Moses was the parter of the waters; now Gabriel is the agent of the miracle."

"Then the Israelites walked dry-shod through the deep; now the Virgin bore the Christ without seed. Note the marvelous ringing of the changes as it were: "After Israel's crossing the sea remained impassable; after Emmanuel's birth the blameless one remained involate." *he thalassa -- he amemptos, Israel, Emmanuel, avatos, aphthros.*

The last example, also drawing on the Red Sea typology, is the first Ode of the Canon for the Feast of the Exaltation of the Precious Cross, known familiarly by its opening words: *Stauron charaxas*. Striking a straight line with his staff, Moses split the Red Sea to let Israel cross on foot. Straightforward enough. But then it gets complicated. *Ten de epistreptikos, Pharao tois armasi krotesas henwsen.*

Ten de refers again to the staff. But what exactly does *epistreptikos* mean? After considerable digging one discovers that the poet is employing a military, or martial, figure. It means a second blow, a return strike, literally at right angles to the first. It is not unlike the "thrust and parry" in a sword fight. But for the poet it is of the most vital (crucial?) significance: Then, smiting it (the Sea) at right angle, he closed it again over Pharaoh's chariots. Thus he described a broad image of the invincible weapon, the Cross.

Such, then, is the task of preservation through translation. The structures must be maintained in their full integrity, for is not Christ the cornerstone? They are the place of encounter with the dive; we come and go in them – Vespers and Matins, Compline and Paraclesis – to be sheltered and comforted and sanctified. To them we bring, figuratively as well as literally, the best we have, for in fact we have nothing. Only what is already God's. *Ta Sa ek ton Son*, we say as we make our offerings.

The Orthodox doctrine of the Incarnation is not that the King of Glory "emptied Himself," to be born in a stable and laid where animals eat, and that therefore all that pertains to our worship must be crude and humble. His coming to our world, His world, to walk the dusty back streets of the human condition of the whole of Creation the deification, or divinization, of man.

As the devout Orthodox housewife prepares her altar bread, her "Prosphora," making certain that she is both bodily and spiritually cleansed; as we bring to the Church the best of everything we have – virgin olive oil for the lamps, the finest wine for communion, the most fragrant incense; as the priest vests himself fittingly for the Sacrifice; as the signers offer their most sublime music – so in all things, surely not least in the words of praise and adoration, all is directed to the celestial altar, as an offering of spiritual fragrance, with this sole hope: that He will in turn send down upon us the grace of the Holy Spirit.

Orthodox Eve and Her Church

Eva Catafygiotu Topping

She is far beyond the price of pearls. Give her a share in what her hands have made. Let her works tell her praises.
Proverbs 31:10,31

It is said that an old lady once complained, "I don't know what I think until I hear what I say." Be this story apocryphal or true, I am not like that old lady. Before you and I hear what I am about to say, I already know what I think about Orthodox Eve and her church. Plainly put – it is that the church has erred in its traditional theology and practices regarding women and that the time has come for a turn-around or conversion, what in Greek is called *metanoia*.

For the past several years I have been studying, speaking and writing about the history and status of women in the Orthodox Church.[1] In the course of research in the original sources I have literally immersed myself in Greek texts. I am forever reading the Bible in Greek; sermons and commentaries by Greek church fathers and theologians; the Greek lives of saints; and the vast multi-volume treasure of Byzantine hymns. Hymns

---

[1] See the collection of essays in my book *Holy Mothers of Orthodoxy: Women and the Church* (Minneapolis, 1987). Henceforth to be cited as *Holy Mothers*.

to the Theotokos and women saints number in the thousands.

In fact, my interest in Orthodox Eve and her church has its genesis in Greek hymnography. To this birthright Greek Orthodox woman the hymns were a revelation. In them I discovered the spiritual core that distinguishes the Orthodox faith from that of the other branches of Christianity. This illuminating core consists first, of the belief in God *Philanthropos*, a compassionate parent, physician, teacher and friend who loves people indiscriminately; and second, the belief in the deification (*theosis*) of every person, female and male alike. Orthodoxy teaches that the divine image and likeness exists equally in both sexes; that women and men can become God. Here in Orthodoxy's charter beliefs no gender discrimination exists.

Yet in the same hymns I discovered a full-blown ideology which consistently demeans and denigrates women.[2] Even the holiest women saints are not exempted from the stigma of being female. These holy mothers of our church are routinely praised for having transcended the generic handicaps of the female sex and for having achieved manhood.[3] This startling contradiction between Orthodoxy's fundamental teachings and its view of women piqued my interest, personal as well as scholarly.

I know of no subject more fascinating and challenging than Orthodox Eve and her church. Furthermore, it poses a prob-

---

[2] Discussed in Eva C. Topping, "Patriarchal Prejudice and Pride in Greek Christianity: Some Notes on Origins." *Journal of Modern Greek Studies I* (1983), pp. 7-17, reprinted in *Holy Mothers*, pp. 45-55.

[3] For example, St. Eudokia (March 1) is eulogized for "preaching like a man;" St. Eugenia (December 24) for turning to "male activities" like "explaining to everyone the truth of the Scriptures;" St. Katherine the great Martyr for "changing the weakness of female nature to masculinity."

lem critical of the present and future spiritual welfare of our church. The re-definition of woman and the expansion of her role and participation in the rich liturgical and sacramental life of the church and its ministry (*diakonia*) demand our serious attention. The existence and urgency of this problem can no longer be either flatly denied, evaded by double-speak obfuscations or explained away by novel doctrines unknown to the church fathers.

Orthodox women do not constitute a "minority" or "special interest group." From the beginning women were and still are more than half of the *ekklesia*. When next in church, look around you. Although you will see only males at the altar, you will quickly see that females outnumber males in the congregation. Yet almost always the congregation is addressed as "brethren," although women are obviously not "brothers."[4]

The women of our church experience in their lives the contradictions evidenced in the hymns. One simple illustration. Recently a notice, repeated four times in my parish bulletin, began with this sentence: "All young men between the ages 10-18 are invited to serve in the Holy Altar."[5] Four times it painfully reminded *all* young women between the ages 10-18 that they will never receive such an invitation. For no reason other than that they are females, they are denied the joy and privilege of serving God at the altar. For older women it is just one more reminder of the discrimination we, our mothers and foremothers have experienced for almost 2000 years.

All Orthodox women know that gender discrimination lasts

---

[4] The ecclesial invisibility of Orthodox women could be easily lessened by the use of inclusive language.

[5] The priest sadly reported later that only three young men responded to the four appeals. It is, of course, unknown how many young women would have accepted the invitation. My guess is the number would have been higher than three.

a life-time. Exclusion from the Holy Altar begins very early, when we are just 40 days old. At the traditional 40 day blessing the priest carries the male infant inside the Royal Gates and around the altar. At 40 days the male gains permanent access to holy space. On the other hand, the female infant is carried only as far as the iconostasis. She is thus denied entry into sacred space. The denial is permanent. Her exclusion last forever.[6]

The relevant canons notwithstanding, no one would argue that the 40 day-old female infant is less holy, less pure, less innocent than the 40 day-old male infant. Would anyone argue seriously that she is created less in the image and likeness of God? Why, then, are the two equally precious babies treated differently? Unpleasant and painful though it may be, the plain truth of the matter is that the discrimination against tiny 40 day-old Orthodox Eve is based on sex.

Although at 40 days we are unaware of sexist bias, we unhappily experience it soon enough, at critical points of physical and emotional development and fulfillment. During menstrual periods and for 40 days after giving birth Orthodox Eve is considered "unclean" and is denied communion and participation in the sacraments.[7] Based on fear and ignorance of the life-giving processes operative in the female body, this primi-

---

[6] See *Holy Mothers*, pp. 126-128. It was heartening to read in *The Orthodox Church* (November 1988) that in India the Malankara Orthodox Syrian Church has changed certain liturgical practices in order to enhance the role of women. Now girls as well as boys are taken around the altar and women are reading the lessons from the Bible in the liturgy.

[7] In June 1986 a prominent Greek Orthodox theologian wrote these shocking words to describe a new mother: "Uncleanliness is a description of her biological condition." By the fortieth day, he continued, she has "normalized" and can return to "normal social and church life." One is forced to ask whether it is his view or that of the church that it is "abnormal" for a woman to give birth to another image of God.

tive taboo is still defended and generally enforced. Despite the repeated proclamations by church spokesmen (and some spokeswomen) that motherhood is woman's supreme vocation,[8] to give birth is still considered "physically unclean" and "ritually impure."

Equally ironic is the fact that Christ himself rejected the traditional blood taboo when he healed the hemorrhaging woman. The three Synoptic Gospels all tell this wonderful story.[9] Yet our church continues to ignore its teaching of liberation and the practice of its founder.

Given life-long experience of inequality in the church, Orthodox women are now just beginning to question our restricted "place" within the *ekklesia*. On this important matter, our Jewish, Catholic and Protestant sisters have moved far ahead of us. Already there are ordained women rabbis. The title of a book *New Catholic Women*[10] needs no explanation. It will, alas, be a long time before a book titled *New Orthodox Women* can be written. The Anglican Communion has ordained women priests and recently elected its first woman bishop.[11]

Whenever Orthodox Eve dares to ask why she does not

[8] It is worth noting that I have yet to find a paean to motherhood in the writings of the Greek church fathers. Glowing encomia to motherhood are a fairly recent phenomenon.

[9] *Mark 5:25-34; Matthew 9:20-22; Luke 8:43-48.* The unnamed woman of the Gospels is venerated by the Orthodox Church as St. Veronike (July 12).

[10] Written by Dr. Mary Jo Weaver, associate professor of religious studies at Indiana University, this informative work was published in San Francisco, 1987.

[11] The first woman Anglican priest was ordained in 1944 in China. Since 1974 about a thousand women priests have been ordained by the Episcopal Church in the United States. The first woman bishop was elected in the Episcopal Diocese of Boston in the fall of 1988 and will be enthroned February 1989. The Methodist Church has already elevated women to the episcopacy.

share the status and privileges of Orthodox Adam, the standard answer is "tradition." Furthermore, she is sternly told that the "tradition" concerning women is spelled with a capital "T." Hence, discussion is ruled out of order. As for change, that is unthinkable. The authority of the Greek church fathers is also invoked. Of course, no proper pious Orthodox woman should think of challenging them. Thus far, these stonewalling tactics have seldom failed to intimidate and prevent discussion.

Consequently, Orthodox Eve remains in the dark about the origins of the tradition spelled with a capital "T" and about the premises on which the church fathers created it. For example, she does not know that this untouchable "tradition" categorically *mandates* second-class status for women in both society and church. One of Orthodoxy's most prestigious theologians, St. Cyril, Patriarch of Alexandria, expressed patristic consensus when he wrote 1500 years ago, "the male must always be in command and the female in second class (*en deftera taxei*) everywhere."[12] A more honest declaration of universal male supremacy and female subservience is hard to imagine. Unlike contemporary hierarchs and theologians who beat around the bush, Cyril, to his credit, tells it "like it is." This patriarch, it should be noted, combined profound devotion to the Theotokos with deep contempt for all other women.[13]

Were St. Cyril to descend from heaven today for a pastoral visit, the sight of women at the seminary, in archdiocesan of-

---

[12] Migne, *Patrologia Graeca* 68. 1068C. Henceforth to be cited as *Migne*.

[13] Mary's most fervent champion, Cyril dominated the Council of Ephesus (431), which declared her Theotokos. Despite the fact that he was the contemporary and fellow townsman of Hypatia, the renowned Alexandrian philosopher and mathematician, Cyril believed women were intellectually inferior to men. Contemporary historians implicated him in the murder of Hypatia by monks in March 415, during Lent.

fices and parish councils would cause him severe cultural shock. Once, however, he realized that they were mostly token women, none of whom hold positions of authority, he would quickly recover. Cyril could then return to his celestial mansion, happy that despite enormous scientific advances and socio-economic changes, the patriarchal structures of his day survive intact in his church; and satisfied that power still rests in the hands of the all-male ordained clergy and that women are *en deftera taxei*, exactly where he has long ago consigned them.

Likewise, stonewalling tactics prevent Orthodox Eve from learning about the two basic assumptions by which Cyril and the other Greek fathers justified and mandated women's secondary status, our permanent subordination to men.

First, the founding fathers of Christianity, East and West, assumed that inferiority of the female sex was designed by God and forever set in eternal concrete. *Genesis* 2[14] provided them with biblical authority for this dubious premise. God created Eve, the first woman, from a rib which Adam luckily could spare. Thus, women are derivative creatures, secondary to and dependent on men. Theologians and hymnographers sometimes refer to Eve and her daughters simply as "the rib." This term clearly dehumanizes women, and denies our personhood. Adam is *the* human being, while Eve is somehow less than a whole person.

Inevitably, inferiority signifies weakness. Clement of Alexandria, the second-century erudite Christian philosopher and teacher, explains that when God removed a rib from Adam to create Eve, God "purged the male of all softness and weakness."[15] Weakness was transferred *in toto* to the first woman and then exclusively to her female descendents everafter.

In both sermons and hymns I have encountered more times

[14] This aetiological folk-tale is the older of the two creation accounts in *Genesis*.
[15] *Migne* 8:58 1A-B. Clement also claimed that man's beard

than I can possibly count the phrase "the weakness of women" (*astheneia*). The more colorful stronger descriptions of "emptiness" and "rottenness" (*to sathron*) sometimes replace the word "weakness."[16]

In *I Peter* 3:7, the fathers found a second text to their liking. Women are here designated "the weaker vessel" (*to asthenesteron skevos*). The author of this influential text cannot be credited with originality. The idea of female inferiority and weakness had been current in the Mediterranean world many centuries before Plato and Aristotle gave it philosophical and "scientific" respectability. To be specific, Aristotle taught that women are basically "deformed males."[17] Eight centuries later, a Christian presbyter in Asia Minor, the author of *I Peter* 3:7, elevated an ancient pagan sexist view of women into the eternal word of God.

By the fifth century the Greek church fathers had fleshed out in precise and occasionally picturesque detail a durable icon of the "weaker vessel." According to these men, the innate *astheneia* of women is more than physical. We are alleged to be emotionally, morally and intellectually "weaker" than men. A

proved his superiority. Although he admitted women to the famous catechetical school which he directed, Clement nevertheless considered spinning and weaving more compatible with women's limited intellectual capacities. See George H. Tavard, *Women in Christian Tradition* (Notre Dame and London, 1973), pp. 62-66, for a useful discussion of Clement's views.

[16] For example, a Byzantine hymnographer hails St. Marina the Great Martyr (July 17) as "marvelous" because she "strengthened female rottenness." Such backhanded compliments appear regularly in hymns to the most honored female saints.

[17] *De Generatione Animalium* 782A. 17ff. For an analysis of Aristotle's widespread influence see Vern Bullough. "Medieval Medical and Scientific Views of Women," *Viator* 4 (1973), pp. 485-501. See also Vern L. Bullough, Brenda Shelton and Sarah Slavian, *The Subordinated Sex. A History of Attitudes Towards Women*, revised edition (Athens GA and London, 1988), pp. 53-55.

few examples will illustrate the fathers' views on women. St. Epiphanios of Cyprus attributed to women instability, frenzy, weak-mindedness and vanity.[18] St. Gregory the Theologian ascribed to women ostentation and self-indulgence.[19] St. Cyril believed that women's powers of understanding were defective.[20]

St. John Chrysostom eloquently described women as "naturally" servile, superficial, fickle, garrulous and lacking the capacity to reason.[21] Invoking the unimpeachable authority of the Apostle Paul, he summarizes "female nature" in one familiar word — *vlakeia* (stupidity).[22] Hence, Chrysostom concludes, women should be confined to unimportant, undemanding domestic roles.[23] He applauds this gender-role arrangement because it frees men to conduct the important affairs of church and state.

Although the repetition of these ideas in the Greek sources soon grows tiresome, they should not be lightly dismissed, or laughed at. Their influence on the lives of generations of Orthodox women can never be measured. Nor, unfortunately, have these ideas become a relic of remote times.[24] As the novelist

[18] *Migne*, 42. 740D, 745B. This fourth-century episcopal misogynist and hunter of heresies credited Eve with the first heresy (*ibid.* 750D-753A).

[19] *Migne*, 35. 800.

[20] According to Cyril "the whole species of females is somewhat slow of understanding" (*Migne*, 74. 689B, 691C-692-D).

[21] *Migne*, 47. 510-511; 59. 346; 61.316; 62.548.

[22] A. Wenger, a.a., *Jean Chrysostome. Huit catéchèses baptismales inédites* (Paris, 1957), p. 126. This word resonates with contempt for women.

[23] *Migne*, 62. 500. For fuller discussion and references consult Elizabeth A. Clark, *Jerome, Chrysostom and Friends* (New York and Toronto, 1979), pp. 1-34. The "friends" referred to in the title were all aristocratic women.

[24] In our own century a Russian Orthodox theologian declared that

William Faulkner observed, it is true that "The past is never over. It isn't even past."

The sinfulness of women is the second and equally important assumption of the fathers concerning the nature (*physis*) of women. First in the order of sin, and second in the order of nature, Eve bequeathed a crippling legacy to all her daughters, the one exception being the woman chosen to carry God in her womb.

Mary's unique destiny separates her from all other women. Significantly, Mary is described as "the descendent of Adam" rather than the daughter of Eve. Theologians and church poets delighted in contrasting Eve and Mary, setting the notorious imperfections of the "first mother" against the ineffable perfection of God's All-Holy mother. The chasm separating the Theotokos from the rest of her sex is emphasized repeatedly in Byzantine hymns and manifested architecturally as well. In Orthodox churches a large imposing image of the Virgin Mother, located in the apse, dominates the holy space around the altar. Since the space in front of her is strictly for men only, she stands alone in majestic isolation from her sisters. Statements to the contrary notwithstanding, the high honor accorded to Mary by our church has yet to trickle down to Orthodox Eve.[25]

Biblical authority for the unique sinfulness of women comes from *Genesis* 3. Gullible, weak-minded Eve disobeyed God and

woman is a "vessel of infirmity" characterized by "inadequate self-control, irresponsibility, passion, blind judgments." Quoted from *A Treasury of Russian Spirituality*, ed. G. P. Fedotov (New York, 1965), p.430.

[25] The deeply felt veneration of the Theotokos, evidenced in liturgy, hymnography, iconography and the piety of the faithful, has given Orthodoxy a "feminine face." The same is true of Roman Catholicism. See Rosemary Radford Ruether, *The Feminine Face of the Church* (Philadelphia, 1977).

became the first sinner in human history. Adam's part in the catastrophic event in Eden is on the whole conveniently over-looked.[26] Moreover, as woman's first victim, he becomes the object of sympathy. One Byzantine hymnwriter wistfully regrets that the first sample of the "stronger" sex "obeyed his rib."

Responsibility for the loss of paradise is thus pinned solely on Eve, with dire and lasting consequences for women. "Sin" (*amartia*) has ever since been tied to the first woman and her sex.[27] During Great Lent, the season for repentance and conversion, women are primarily paradigms of sinners. Eve, the "sinful woman" of *Luke* 7:36-50, and St. Mary of Egypt, a reformed harlot,[28] dominate Lenten sermons and hymns. The most beloved of these hymns is Kassiane's troparion, "The Woman Fallen into Many Sins."[29] Reading these Lenten texts, one would never guess that men, just as often as women, also fall into many sins, and that most of the time they sin together. The harsh accent of "sin," however, falls conspicuously on women.

By the time of Saints Cyril and Chrysostom the powerful

[26] The exoneration of Adam begins in *I Timothy* 2:14.

[27] Seen through androcentric lenses, sin has no "father," only a well-publicized "mother." The Greek Church fathers consistently branded Eve as the "mother" or "author" of sin. See, for example, Theophilos of Antioch (*Migne*, 6. 1096A); St. Athanasius of Alexandria (*Migne*, 27. 240D).

[28] The most celebrated of all our harlot-saints, Mary of Egypt is commemorated three times each year, April 1, the Fifth Thursday and Sunday of Lent. Other haloed harlots include Taisia and Pelagia of Antioch (October 8); Maria the Niece of Abraham (October 29); Akylina and Kallinike (May 9).

[29] See Eva C. Topping, "Kassiane the Nun and the Sinful Woman," *Greek Orthodox Theological Review* 16 (1981), pp. 201-209, reprinted in *Holy Mothers*, pp. 30-38; "The Psalmist, St. Luke and Kassia the Nun," *Byzantine Studies/Etudes Byzantines* 9 (1982), pp. 199-210.

tradition spelled with a capital "T" was in place. Built to outlast time, it rests on selected scriptural texts, androcentric exegesis and patriarchal structures in church and society. It rests also on the awesome authority of its creators, the church fathers of the first five Christian centuries.

Designed by men, this tradition defines women as inferior, weaker and more sinful than men and relegates them to permanent second-class status. To our own day it has succeeded in limiting women's roles in the "royal priesthood"[30] to which all Orthodox Christians are called.

For the reasons alleged by this negative tradition, Orthodox Eve is less "royal" than Orthodox Adam. Her sex disqualifies her for the ordained ministry. No ambiguity exists on this point. In his treatise *On the Priesthood* St. John Chrysostom describes the moral, intellectual and pastoral imperatives of the ordained ministry. Quite simply, without mincing words, he twice excludes *all women*[31] from the priesthood. All of them are inferior and have a "propensity to sin." In contrast to *all women, all men* are not subject to these fatal flaws. Therefore, *some* men can become priests. In the same treatise Chrysostom advises priests and bishops that women require greater pastoral care and supervision because of their "propensity to sin."[32]

If there were no alternative to this anti-woman tradition, the future for Orthodox Eve would be as repressive as the past.

---

[30] *I Peter* 2:9. See my essay "Orthodox Eve and the Royal Priesthood" in *Holy Mothers*, pp. 102-121.

[31] W. A. Jurgens, *The Priesthood. A Translation of the Peri Hierosynes of St. John Chrysostom* (New York, 1950), pp. 17, 38. He calls the exclusion a "divine law"(*theos monos*). However, after reading the disparaging remarks made repeatedly by Chrysostom in this treatise (and elsewhere), one concludes that it is rather a law made and perpetuated by *men* who assert superiority and claim domination over women.

[32] *Ibid*, p. 101: *dia to pros tas amartias evolisthon.*

Fortunately for her and her church, an alternate tradition exists, one which affirms women's humanity, our creation in the divine image and likeness. Although it has been neglected and even suppressed, this affirming tradition nevertheless has deep roots both in scriptures and in the historical experience of the *ekklesia.*

Its biblical roots, moreover, were not unknown to the fathers. They were well acquainted with *Genesis* 1:27, which provides theological basis for the equality of the sexes: "So God created man in his image ... male and female he created them." The fathers sometimes quoted this text. It apparently troubled them. However, when it came to formulating the church's view of women, they either ignored it, or postponed its application until the next world. Brilliant and creative thinkers to whom Christianity owes much, the church fathers were nevertheless men of their time, unable to transcend the entrenched patriarchal patterns and anti-woman prejudices of their culture. As a result, they shut and bolted the door to the new creation, in which Christ intended women and men to be equally and fully human.[33]

As depicted in the four Gospels, Jesus offers a new and affirming vision of women. Matthew, Mark, Luke and John record not a single instance in which Jesus demeaned a woman, or prescribed a special "feminine" role for her. On the contrary, the Gospels dramatically record many striking instances of the liberating and empowering grace with which he treated all

---

[33] See Leonard Swidler, "Jesus Was a Feminist," *Catholic World,* January 1971, pp. 177-183. On the first page the author defines a feminist as "a person who is in favor of, and who promotes the equality of women with men, a person who advocates and practices treating women primarily as human persons ... and willingly contravenes social customs in so acting."

women. One has already been mentioned. When Jesus restored the bleeding woman to health and society, he rejected the blood taboo that reduced women to nonbeings. It was certainly his intention to abolish it.[34]

When he welcomed Mary of Bethany into his intimate circle of disciples to study and learn,[35] Christ violated the ancient custom forbidding rabbis to teach women. By sitting "at the Lord's feet" and listening "to his teaching," Mary had assumed a traditional "male" role. But her teacher and friend did not shoo her back to pots and pans in the kitchen, a typical "female" task in patriarchal societies, then and now. Instead, stating that choices also existed for women, Jesus declared that Mary had the right to choose for herself – a revolutionary notion, which in 1988 has yet to be universally accepted. "Mary has chosen the better part; it is not to be taken from her." With these plain words (*Luke* 10:42) God Incarnate not only recognizes but also blesses the autonomy and freedom of women.

In contrast to the fathers, Christ did not believe that women are "weak" in mind and understanding. Indeed, women proved to be more perceptive and responsive than men to his divinity and to his mission of liberation. Why else would Christ have many times revealed his true identity first to women?

One hot noonday, he sat by a well and discussed theology with a Samaritan woman.[36] "God is spirit and whoever wor-

---

[34] See above, note 9.

[35] This story is told in *Luke* 10:38-42. See the interpretation by Elisabeth Moltmann-Wendell, *The Women Around Jesus* (New York, 1982), pp. 51-58.

[36] As recorded in *John* 4:1-30. Christ's dialogue with the Samaritan Woman is his longest conversation. For a discussion of this extraordinary encounter see *Holy Mothers*, pp. 56-58. Known as St. Photeine, the Samaritan Woman is celebrated on February 26 and the Fourth Sunday after Easter. Theologians grant her the title "apostle" and "evangelist;" hymnwriters exalt her as "god-bearing" (*theophoros*).

ships God must worship in the spirit and truth," he told her (*John* 4:24). To this self-confessed adulteress, social outcast, and member of a religious sect despised by Jews, Jesus revealed for the first time that he was the Messiah foretold by the prophets. When the male disciples returned and saw their teacher talking with a woman in public, something no respectable Jewish rabbi ever did, they were "surprised." Had they known what he had just revealed to her, they would have been stunned.

He comforted Martha of Bethany, weeping for her dead brother Lazarus, by revealing to her, "I am the resurrection and the life . . . whoever lives and believes in me shall never die" (*John* 11:25-26). A revelation that was destined to change the world, it was first made to a woman.[37]

Finally, the Risen Lord appeared first to women. Recorded in the Gospels, Christianity's most ancient traditions unanimously agree that St. Mary Magdalene and the Myrrh-bearing Women are the first witnesses of the Resurrection.[38] In Byzantine hymns and sermons again and again these disciples (*mathetriai*) are appropriately named the "first" witnesses and "evangelists." Commissioned by the Risen Lord himself to announce his *anastas* (resurrection) to the frightened male disciples, St. Mary Magdalene, the most faithful of all the disciples, is honored as the "apostle to the apostles."[39]

[37] Jesus' disclosure and Martha's confession are related in *John* 11:17-27. See Leonard Swidler, *Biblical Affirmations of Woman* (Philadelphia, 1979), pp. 216-218. Henceforth this useful work will be cited as *Biblical Affirmations*.

[38] *Mark* 16:1-11; *Matthew* 28:1-10; *Luke* 24;1-11; *John* 20:1-18. The Myrrh-bearing Women are celebrated on the Second Sunday after Easter and in many hundreds of paschal hymns.

[39] Mentioned twelve times in the Gospels, Mary Magdalene is clearly a major figure in the group that gathered around Jesus and shared in his ministry. See *Holy Mothers*, p. 70.; *Biblical Affirmations*, pp. 204-214; Rosemary Radford Ruether, *Sexism and*

Described in the Gospels as the only true disciples of Christ, these women constitute a holy icon of superhuman faith, loyalty and courage. As for the sacrosanct all-male "Twelve" (spelled with a capital "T"), theirs is a spectacle of sorry weakness. One of them, Judas, betrayed Jesus for a few pieces of silver. Another, Peter, frightened by a slave girl, denied him three times. And all the male disciples fled and abandoned their teacher at the time of his arrest.[40] Only the women remained with him all the way, from the crucifixion to the tomb and beyond. Once again, the "weaker vessel" had turned out after all to be the stronger.

Extraordinary as it is to contemplate, the fundamental Christian *kerygma*, the resurrection of Jesus from the dead, rests ultimately on the word and witness of women. From their lips fell the first joyful words, "Christ is Risen" (*Christos Aneste*).[41] Without the witness of these *women* there would be no Easter story to proclaim. To understand how radical is this acceptance of their word, we need only note that in the days of St. Mary Magdalene women were not allowed to testify in Jewish courts. A woman's word was automatically not worth hearing.

This equal discipleship of women and men which existed in the community gathered around Jesus continued in the primitive church. According to the New Testament, women apostles, prophets, teachers and deacons, along with men, ex-

---

God-Talk: Toward a Feminist Theology (Boston, 1983), pp. 8-11. The memory of this extraordinary woman is celebrated in the Orthodox Church on July 22. Byzantine hymns honoring St. Mary Magdalene preserve the tradition of her prominence among the disciples and in the apostolic church. I have underway a study of these important and revealing hymns.

[40] In a brief statement, *Mark* 14:50 describes the abandonment of Jesus by his male disciples: *kai afentes auton efygon pantes*

[41] See *Holy Mothers*, pp. 68-69.

ercised leadership in the apostolic church. Within the body of Christ discrimination based on race, sex, or social class seems not to have existed then. The more reason it should not exist today. In the ringing words of St. Paul, "All of you who have been baptized in Christ have clothed yourselves in Christ. There is neither Jew nor Greek, slave nor free, male nor female."[42] Proclaimed as a basic principle in this ancient baptismal formula, the promise of ecclesial equality for women still remains unfulfilled in our church.

The names of women church leaders preserved in Acts and the Epistles testify to equal discipleship in the early Christian communities. The pen of the Apostle Paul inscribed many of them on the pages of ecclesiastical history. In the remarkable sixteenth chapter of *Romans*,[43] Paul salutes no fewer than ten prominent churchwomen: Phoebe, Prisca, Mariam, Jounia, Tryphaina, Tryphosa, Persis, the mother of Rufus, Julia and the sister of Nereus. This catalogue not only confirms the numerically significant presence of women in the early church. It also confirms that women held offices, positions of leadership, and were in no way subordinate to their brothers in Christ. They were definitely not *en deutera taxei*.

Phoebe, the deacon of the large church in the port city of Corinth, heads this list. Paul praises her as a "leader over many, indeed over me."[44] He names Jounia, who with her husband is

---

[42] *Galatians* 3:27-28. See *Biblical Affirmations*, pp. 322-323.

[43] See *Holy Mothers*, pp. 142-144.

[44] In *Romans* 16:1-2 Paul calls Phoebe a deacon (*diakonos*) not a *diakonissa*, a word which appeared first in the fourth century. For a discussion of women deacons consult *Biblical Affirmations*, pp. 309-314 and Roger Gryson, *The Ministry of Women in the Early Church* (Collegeville MN, 1980), *passim*.

"distinguished among the apostles."[45] Mentioned six times in the New Testament, Prisca (better known as Priscilla) is the most prominent woman apostle, a brilliant teacher, and one of Paul's most valued and successful collaborators.[46] Elsewhere, he mentions two other women apostles, Apphia (*Philemon* 1-2) and Nympha (*Colossians* 4:15). It is of major significance that the greatest of all apostles (himself not one of the "Twelve") never once suggests that the women apostles are his subordinates. From this we may conclude that their apostolates did not differ from his and that St. Paul actively promoted women's full participation in all forms of ministry.

The Orthodox Church recognizes all these four women as apostles, along with Saints Xanthippe, Polyxene,[47] Photeine the Samaritan Woman,[48] Mary Magdalene, [49] Thekla[50] and

---

[45] *Romans* 16:7. Recognized as *apostolos*, St. Jounia is celebrated on May 17. Unable to accept the historical fact that women are also called apostles, some theologians have arbitrarily changed her name to *Jounias*, an unattested masculine form! See Bernadette Brooten, " 'Junia . . . Outstanding among the Apostles' (*Romans*: 16:)" in *Women Priests. A Catholic Commentary on the Vatican Declaration*, ed. Leonard Swidler and Arlene Swidler (New York, Ramsey and Toronto, 1977), pp. 141-144. In this important work, Catholic theologians reject Rome's arguments against the ordination of women.

[46] *Romans* 16:3; *Acts* 18:2, 18:26; *I Corinthians* 16:19; *II Timothy* 4:18. With one exception, Prisca's name precedes that of her husband. The reversal of the patriarchal order of naming husband and wife indicates that she was the more prominent of the two. On February 13 the Orthodox Church honors St. Priscilla *apostolos*.

[47] September 23

[48] See above note 36.

[49] See above note 39.

[50] September 24. Also honored as the first woman martyr, St. Thekla enjoyed immense popularity in the Byzantine world.

Mariamne, sister of the Apostle Philip.[51] Going back to the very beginnings of the church, this authentic Orthodox tradition preserves the history of women apostles. Leaving behind them the security of conventional domesticity and privacy, these women publicly risked their lives as they traveled from city to city to preach, convert and establish churches in a hostile pagan world. They deserve their haloes and recognition at last of the fact that Christianity has founding mothers as well as founding fathers.

The New Testament also attests that in the primitive church women exercised authority as prophets. When the Holy Spirit touched them with fire and vision, God spoke through women. *Acts* 21:9 refers to the four prophesying daughters of Philip the Evangelist. Hermione, one of this famous quartet, is honored by the Orthodox church as a saint,[52] along with other female prophets from the Old and New Testaments.

In seeking guidance for conversion (*metanoia*) from the traditional negative view of women and from their traditional gender circumscribed "place" in the church, where better to find models than in the transforming grace, attitudes and practices of Christ and the egalitarian first Christian communities.[53]

In addition to the positive tradition documented in the New Testament there exists another one created over many centuries in many lands by many women, young and old, rich

---

[51] February 17. See Eva C. Topping, "St. Joseph the Hymnographer and St. Mariamne Isapostolos," *Byzantina* 13 (1986), pp. 1035-1052.

[52] On September 4 she is celebrated as a prophet, teacher, healer and preacher.

[53] As the Christian communities became progressively institutionalized, women's freedom began to be restricted. In the church's efforts to achieve respectability, patriarchal restrictions were adopted and women's equality disappeared.

and poor, empress and slave, married and single. Proof of this powerful affirming tradition is to be found in Orthodoxy's bright galaxy of women saints.[54] Ten thousand times over, these heroines refute the patriarchal monolithic image of woman as hyper-sinful and as a "weak vessel, a cracked pot."[55] At the same time, they subvert the conventional image of the female saint as meek and mute, submissive and long-suffering.

Holiness knows no gender. The church acknowledges this by admitting women to sainthood. Women travel the exact same routes to heaven and sanctity as do men. Saints in skirts convened and directed ecumenical councils; sought and found God in desert wildernesses; slew dragons and walked on water; discovered relics and founded churches; built and governed convents; performed miracles. Until the twelfth century saints in skirts served God at the altar as ordained deacons. From the earliest days to the present, women endured persecutions and paid blood tribute to our church. Many hundreds of saints in skirts wear the martyr's crown and carry the palm of victory.

A few favorite illustrations from this sacred galaxy. St. Elizabeth the Miracle-Worker,[56] a famous abbess in fifth-century Constantinople, out-Georged St. George. She killed a ferocious dragon by stepping on him with her bare feet. (She never wore shoes, winter or summer.) After making the sign of the cross, she spat on him. And that was the end of the dragon who had long terrorized the imperial capital. Our Holy Mother Elizabeth had no need of a horse or any lethal military weapons. Non-violence, faith and holiness served her better.

---

[54] A few examples are given in *Holy Mothers*, pp. 71-80.

[55] From *Les Homélies festales d'Hesychius de Jérusalem I*, ed. M. Aubineau (Brussels, 1978), p. 26.

[56] Her feast day falls on April 24. For an account of her life, see F. Halkin, "Sainte Elisabeth d'Héraclée, Abbesse à Constantinople," *Analecta Bollandiana* 9 (1973), pp. 248-264.

St. Theodosia of Constantinople,[57] an eighth century nun, led a public demonstration against the emperor's policy outlawing the veneration of icons. She and the women with her caused the death of an imperial officer when they tried to prevent the desecration of a famous icon of Christ. Theodosia, the ringleader, was arrested. After enduring brutal tortures, she was martyred for her fidelity to Orthodox tradition.

The Holy Martyr Philothea of Athens,[58] an aristocratic sixteenth-century abbess, dedicated talents, fortune and life to the preservation of Hellenism and Orthodoxy in Turkish-ruled Greece. Her philanthropic institutions included a school for girls, a hospital, a shelter for the homeless and a home for the aged. The fearless protector of Greek women in a city ruled by foreigners, Philothea herself became a marked woman. Severely beaten by Turks, the sixty-seven year old abbess died on February 19, 1589, a "holy and blessed mother" of Orthodoxy.

Two spectacular saints belong to the month of November. All-Wise, All-Glorious Great-Martyr St. Katherine of Alexandria[59] offers Orthodox women a unique symbol of intellectual superiority. She commanded classical and Christian learning, had exceptional oratorical skills and knew all the known languages and dialects of that day. At age eighteen, beautiful and

---

[57] The first martyr in the iconoclastic struggle, Theodosia was soon recognized as a saint and quickly became a role model for activist Orthodox women. She is commemorated on May 29. See *Holy Mothers*, pp. 136-137. Despite the blood tribute and sacrifices of many women in the defense of the veneration of icons, each year on the Sunday of Orthodoxy the procession of icon-bearers is all male. Such processions distort the historical record and ignore women's contributions to the victory of 843.

[58] Philothea is the best known of the women who are honored as neo-martyrs. See *Holy Mothers*, pp. 134-135. 1989 will mark the four hundredth anniversary of her martyrdom.

[59] November 25. See *Holy Mothers*, pp. 95-96.

scholarly Katherine publicly debated and defeated the 150 most skilled and wisest pagan philosophers of Alexandria. Enraged by her triumph, the Roman ruler of the city ordered her death. Converted by the learned Christian maiden, the ruler's wife shared Katherine's martyrdom.

Our Holy Mother Matrona of Perge[60] I first encountered in a hymn which enthusiastically praises her for wearing men's clothing and "acquiring the mind of a man." Abandoning husband and child, she became an exemplary monk in a Constantinopolitan male monastery. After the discovery of Matrona's true identity, she spent a number of years as an ascetic in Syria, where she gained fame as a charismatic healer and holy woman. On her return to the imperial city, Matrona attracted a following of wealthy women, and founded a convent. Its prestigious abbess for seventy years, she was a spiritual powerhouse in Constantinople, even though she and her nuns always dressed like monks.

No man or woman who reads the engrossing lives of Orthodoxy's women saints finds it possible to accept the patriarchal definition of women as the more sinful and "weaker vessel." Our haloed heroines subvert this ideology. Far beyond any reasonable doubt, they prove that much-maligned Eve and her daughters are indeed persons created in the divine image and likeness, no less than Adam and his sons.

By now it should be clear that this alternative tradition which affirms women is neither foreign nor extraneous to Orthodoxy. On the contrary, this authentic tradition accords completely with Orthodoxy's profound belief in the goodness of the Creator and of all God's human creatures.

---

[60] November 9. I discuss her remarkable career in "St. Matrona and her Friends: Sisterhood in Byzantium," in *KATHEGETRIA Essays Presented to Joan Hussey*, ed. J. Chrysostomides (London, 1988), pp. 211-224.

Likewise, it should be clear that the positive tradition just described has tremendous significance and implications for Orthodox Eve in 1988. It supports her quest for full dignity and equality in the church. It empowers her for the inevitable long struggle ahead. It informs Orthodox Eve that despite the limitations placed on her by patriarchal prejudice and pride, hers is a proud and illustrious history in her church.

Most importantly, this tradition emphasizes Christ's vision of equal discipleship and equal *diakonia*, a service to God and humankind. It presents a genuinely Christian vision of the new order in which the concept of *deutera taxis* is obsolete; in which there is neither Greek nor Jew, slave nor free, male nor female, and in which Orthodoxy's God of life and love is worshiped in truth and spirit.

Again, I know what I think before I hear what I say. This I know for sure. In the struggle for equal discipleship and *diakonia*, strength, grace and blessings will come to us abundantly from Saints Mary Magdalene, Photeine, Martha and Mary of Bethany, Jounia, Phoebe, Priscilla, Mary of Egypt, Elizabeth, Theodosia, Philothea, Katherine, Matrona and from all our Holy Mothers. Communion with them is part of our heritage as Orthodox women.

Orthodox Eve belongs to a venerable, powerful and sacred sisterhood. Our Orthodox saints, our own mothers and foremothers were strong women. Without their sacrifices, love and loyalty there would be no Orthodox Church today, here or anywhere else.

It remains now for Orthodox Eve to claim equality for herself and at last to take her rightful place in the church to which she has been more than faithful for two thousand long years.